Students a

D.

Urban Economics:
Processes and Problems

Introduction to Economics Series

Kenyon A. Knopf, Editor

NATIONAL INCOME AND EMPLOYMENT ANALYSIS, 2ND. ED.
Arnold Collery

THE MARKET SYSTEM, 2ND. ED.
Robert H. Haveman and Kenyon A. Knopf

INTERNATIONAL ECONOMIC PROBLEMS, 2ND. ED.
James C. Ingram

THE ECONOMICS OF POVERTY, 2ND. ED.
Alan B. Batchelder

THE ECONOMICS OF THE PUBLIC SECTOR
Robert H. Haveman

ECONOMIC DEVELOPMENT AND GROWTH, 2ND. ED. (1972)
Robert E. Baldwin

CASE STUDIES IN AMERICAN INDUSTRY, 2ND. ED.
Leonard W. Weiss

TOWARD ECONOMIC STABILITY
Maurice W. Lee

WELFARE AND PLANNING: AN ANALYSIS OF CAPITALISM VERSUS SOCIALISM
Heinz Kohler

URBAN ECONOMICS
William L. Henderson and Larry C. Ledebur

Urban Economics:
Processes and Problems

WILLIAM L. HENDERSON
LARRY C. LEDEBUR
Denison University, Granville, Ohio

John Wiley & Sons, Inc.
New York · London · Sydney · Toronto

Library of Congress Cataloging in Publication Data

Henderson, William Leroy, 1927–
   Urban economics.

   (Introduction to economics series)
   1. Urban economics.   2. Urbanization.   3. Municipal services.   I. Ledebur, Larry C., joint author. II. Title.

HT321.H4   330.9173'2   75–38935
ISBN 0–471–37044–4
ISBN 0–471–37045–2 (pbk.)

Printed in the United States of America.

10 9 8 7 6 5 4 3 2 1

Introduction to Economics Series

Teachers of introductory economics seem to agree on the impracticality of presenting a comprehensive survey of economics to freshmen or sophomores. Many of them believe there is a need for some alternative which provides a solid core of principles while permitting an instructor to introduce a select set of problems and applied ideas. This series attempts to fill that need and also to give the interested layman a set of self-contained books that he can absorb with interest and profit, without assistance.

By offering greater flexibility in the choice of topics for study, these books represent a more realistic and reasonable approach to teaching economics than most of the large, catchall textbooks. With separate volumes and different authors for each topic, the instructor is not as tied to a single track as in the omnibus introductory economics text.

Underlying the series is the pedagogical premise that students should be introduced to economics by learning how economists think about economic problems. Thus the concepts and relationships of elementary economics are presented to the student in conjunction with a few economic problems. An approach of this kind offers a good beginning to the student who intends to move on to advanced work and furnishes a clearer understanding for those whose study of economics is limited to an introductory exposure. Teachers and students alike should find the books helpful and stimulating.

Kenyon A. Knopf, Editor

Preface

The majority of our population now live in cities. It is projected that the zenith of this centralization process will be a continuous corridor of urbanization across regions—a labyrinth of criss-crossing bands of urbanization spanning continents and national boundaries which will be socially, economically and, perhaps, politically interrelated.

Despite the long historical growth of cities and today's myriad of urban problems, we know comparatively little about our cities and the urbanization process. Only in the post-World War II period have economists systematically begun to study the economics of the city, primarily in response to the rise in urban problems.

Extensive research is now being conducted on urban economic problems and processes. This field, however, is still characterized by inadequate knowledge, an absence of expertise, and too few teaching scholars, teaching materials, and urban economics courses.

As a result of inadequate knowledge and research the process of urban decision making is complex and imprecise. This imprecision is compounded by the methods of policy decision making. Elected city officials and their electorale who ultimately make the decisions regarding the urban environment, do not have access to adequate conceptual tools and analytical frameworks. The training and existing educational processes available to city officials typically do not provide information on the economics of the urban environment.

Courses in urban economics have been introduced only recently to college curriculums (at Harvard in 1965 and at M.I.T. in 1967). In colleges that now offer urban economics, the first course is usually at the graduate or advanced undergraduate levels where the majority of college students not concentrating in economics have little contact. Moreover there is typically little urban economics in the basic economics course for the general student to obtain an understanding of the economic environment in which he will probably live and work.

This book provides introductory economics students with a preliminary insight into the economic dynamics of the city and the economic dimensions of its problems and possible remedial solutions. No single volume can do justice to the complexity of the urban organization and the staggering dimensions of urban problems. However, we hope that this book inspires the student's interest in this field and leads him to an awareness of its complexity and problems, and to the recognition that simple solutions will not suffice.

Development of Topics. The organizational theme of this book is expressed by the quotation, "Given a social system or the city, the question of most significance is what monitors and regulates that system to insure beneficial interaction for the 'social good'." Some decision-making procedure must determine the final configuration of the interaction of a complex and bewildering array of variables. The fundamental dilemma in urban environments is what organizing principles can or should be effective to determine the allocation of land, goods, and services and to arbitrate the economic interactions among persons.

Within a market-oriented society, the pricing mechanism performs this allocative function. Part One examines how market forces and pricing mechanism allocate goods and services through space and time. Part Two explores the adequacy of pricing mechanism in achieving socially desirable results. The efficacy of the pricing mechanism in managing urban processes and problems is the unifying theme of this book.

Chapter 1 is a general introduction to the city and the inherent economic issues. Chapter 2 provides a perspective on the history of the city and projections about urbanization in the future. Chapter 3 develops the macroeconomics of the city and a division of economic functions among cities. Chapter 4 examines the microeconomic functions of the city, and the allocation of resources, goods, and services through space and time. Chapter 5 elaborates on situations in which the market system fails to provide an efficient allocation of urban resources and is the basis for problems that are evident in most cities.

Chapter 6 studies the dilemma of urban public finance and the provision of public services. Chapter 7 focuses on urban mobility and transportation—the problems of providing a flow of people and commodities through the city. Chapter 8 evaluates the pre-eminent problem of the provision of adequate urban housing. Chapter 9 describes the economics of the ghetto and alternate remedial policy proposals for improving the quality of life in these areas. Chapter 10 examines the condition of the city in light of a dependence on pricing mechanism. The book concludes with a discussion of the consequences of this market dependence for the future of the city.

We are intellectually indebted to the scholars and practitioners who have contributed to the growing body of literature on the city and urban problems. We hope that our tribute to them will be, in some small way, to interest another generation of students in thinking analytically about the city and these ongoing problems.

WILLIAM L. HENDERSON
LARRY C. LEDEBUR

Acknowledgments

We are grateful to Paul King, Department of Economics, Denison University, for his valuable help in providing ideas and in reviewing portions of the manuscript. We also thank Mrs. Burton Dunfield, Mrs. Gordon Carlson, and Mrs. William Krieger for their excellent typing and clerical assistance.

W.L.H.
L.C.L.

Contents

Urban Economics:
Processes and Problems

PART ONE

Urban Economics—
Processes and Problems

1

Introduction: the City and Economics

The majority of our nation's population live and interact in metropolitan areas, and it is within this environment that man must adjust socially, psychologically, politically, and economically. Contemporary man confronts an urban society.

For an urban society, we know very little about the urbanization process—the centralization of societal and economic functions. Historically our urban policy has been one of laissez faire predicated on the implicit assumption that unplanned and unregulated development dictated by economic, technological, and demographic forces will result in an environment that is in some way best for man. The result has been cities that to a significant degree may be incompatible with the social, psychological and economic needs of urban man.

If urban man is not to be conditioned, manipulated, and frustrated by his environment, he must gain an understanding of the origins and nature of the metropolitan milieu. Such an understanding introduces the possibility that the city of the future could reflect man's rationality and values rather than be the consequence of unregulated market and social forces and an unbridled and burgeoning technology.

A. The Crisis of the City

It is generally accepted that a "crisis" exists in large metropolitan areas. The true nature of this crisis is only vaguely perceived and seldom articulated. Indeed, the vast majority of urban residents live in an affluence and material prosperity unparalleled in history. Thus the crisis for the majority of urban residents is not one of deprivation. However, an actual urban "crisis" does exist, consisting of four significant dimensions.

1. In the midst of growing material prosperity within the urban environment, there exists a growing sense of personal alienation and anonymity. Increasingly, the urban man is psychologically incompatible with his environment.

The problem can be briefly stated. Specialization of activities and of the person is the source of the distinctive contribution that the urban environment makes to the good life. But it is also the source of that condition of cities which renders them least likely to sustain a good life. What specialization offers to the good life is opportunity. Because urban life is specialized it is diverse; a person confronts an unprecedented wealth of opportunities to act, to express himself, to develop his potentialities. What specialization removes from life is community. By promoting the plurality of individual worlds, specialization dissolves the continuity of persons, their sense of living a common and having common concerns. The problem is that of restoring community to the city in such a way that the distinctive contribution of the city life, the wealth of opportunities it offers, is not lost.[1]

2. For many, albeit a minority, the city does not provide material needs. The plight of the residents of our central cities and the social cost that this environment creates for the nation are well known. For those who live in deprivation within the urban environment, there is a crisis in "essential welfare."[2]

3. A crisis in urban environmental quality and urban social institutions exists. Within the city, man's existence and actions are highly interrelated, creating a mutual interdependence of urban residents. This factor gives rise to many external effects within the city which threaten the quality of that environment. In addition, major urban areas in the United States are facing circumstances that are relatively new, although they are fairly common throughout Europe. Those areas' cities are aging. The

---

[1] Lawrence Haworth, *The Good City* (Bloomington: Indiana University Press, 1966), p. 19.
[2] For further development of this argument, see Edward C. Banfield, *The Unheavenly City* (Boston: Little, Brown and Company, 1970), pp. 3–4.

factors of age and physical deterioration create a spectrum of problems for which we have little historical experience. Thus problems of environmental quality and physical deterioration interreact to create conditions in some city areas that are incompatible with the goal of providing for the "good urban life."

4. The political institutions of the city and the institutional relationships between urban governments and state and federal governments were not designed to facilitate the solution of problems of interdependence and the consequences of unregulated, unplanned growth. The policies of most political institutions regarding the regulation of the environment have been extreme laissez faire. As the magnitude and nature of urban crises change, the need for institutional control becomes more significant. A productive and constructive response will require a high degree of flexibility and innovation by urban political institutions. Whether they can respond to derive creative and regenerative solutions to the urban crises well may be the major test of the continuance of cities without progressive deterioration and paralysis. The challenge to the capacity of political institutions to contend successfully with the growing complexity and frustrations of the city represents a major crisis of the urban environment.

B. Economics and Urban Processes

Urban man is basically a social not an economic animal. He exhibits instinctive and culturally developed socializing desires that foster a propensity to aggregate. However, urban man relies on an economic foundation of jobs, income, and services necessary for subsistence in his environment. With a viable economic base, the city can develop cultural, social, and esthetic values and interpersonal activities that provide meaning for human existence. Without a supportive economic structure, these cultural dimensions cannot be realized. The city must provide an effective economic organization to have a viable cultural and social base.[3] Thus it is important that the "city as an economic organization" be understood.

---

[3] Indeed, it can be argued that many of the social problems and crises of the urban environment are directly related to an inadequate or declining

The understanding of the city as an economic entity can be developed only through the systematic study and application of economic theory to the processes of urbanization. Theoretical analysis and empirical economic studies must be employed to construct an economic theory applicable to the urban environment (Figure 1-1). The foundation of an analytical framework

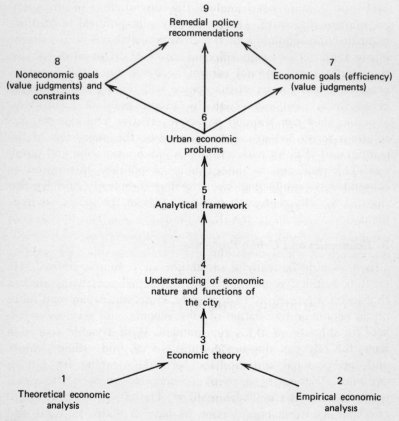

9
Remedial policy
recommendations

8
Noneconomic goals
(value judgments) and
constraints

7
Economic goals (efficiency)
(value judgments)

6
Urban economic
problems

5
Analytical framework

4
Understanding of economic
nature and functions of
the city

3
Economic theory

1
Theoretical economic
analysis

2
Empirical economic
analysis

Figure 1–1

economic base. The inability of the central city of some large metropolitan areas to absorb the excess of or structurally incompatible labor is evidence of a declining economic base.

permits a meaningful examination of urban problems and the design of effective remedial policies. At the level of policy determination, economic analysis must be related to similar analysis in other disciplines. For example, in the derivation of policy, economic objectives such as efficiency will interact with other noneconomic goals that constrain the implementation and direction of policy.

As an economist with an urban focus or as an urbanologist with an economic focus analyzes the city, he becomes quickly aware that the problems of the city relate to the "classical" problems of economics.[4]
The question of *economic efficiency* lies behind many of the controversies concerning the establishment of priorities and the utilization of resources in the urban environment. The question of *equity or distributive* justice underlies many of the pressing problems of housing, jobs, poverty, and urban public finance. Questions of *economic stability* and *economic growth* are at the basis of urban problems such as unemployment, unstable public revenue patterns, low incomes, and a spectrum of urban problems resulting from an inadequate or a declining economic base. In addition, questions of welfare and the quality of life are currently being focused on as an urban problem. Economics is less well equipped to handle these questions, although the analytical framework of social costs and benefits or external cost-benefits provides useful tools for identifying them.[5]

I. URBAN ECONOMICS: THE STATE OF THE ART

For the student of the city, urban economics is a new and underdeveloped discipline. The body of literature is inadequate in terms of empirical studies and theoretical constructs for building a relevant framework of economic analysis. Kenneth Boulding observes that although it is clear that the discipline of economics is making a contribution, it has had two rather conspicuous failures. The first is the failure to derive a good

---

[4] See Harvey S. Perloff and Lowdon Wingo, Jr., "Introduction" in *Issues in Urban Economics* (Baltimore: Johns Hopkins Press, 1968), p. 3.
[5] These questions and decision-making apparatus are examined in Chapter 4.

theory of economic development for underdeveloped countries, and:

The second failure of economics is in the field of urban poverty and deterioration and the whole matter of a provision of a decent physical environment. The defect here I suspect is more of a failure to allocate intellectual resources properly within the economic profession than it is a failure to integrate with other social sciences . . . . The plain fact is that even when it comes to economics, within the narrow framework of such problems as real estate, land speculation, transportation, and tax systems which are clearly within the general preview of the discipline of economics, we find a serious lack not only of theory but, more importantly, of data. What might be called the economic dynamics or the economic ecology of the city is something that has been given shockingly little attention.[6]

There is much to be learned and understood about the economics of urban areas. The difficulty is magnified by the complex interaction of social forces within the city. A broad spectrum of processes and problems exists in which economic concepts interact with the concepts of other disciplines to provide meaningful approaches to understanding the city and its problems. The challenge of urban economics is to derive a meaningful framework for the analysis of the urban economic environment which incorporates an interdisciplinary approach to the study and planning of the city with the design of effective remedial policies for the problems of the urban environment.

The urgent nature of the policy issues arising in urban areas has stimulated the rapid development of the field of urban economics.

In the case of urban economics, the history of the field can be represented in the following developmental sequence. There are a number of pressing, practical urban problems for which policies must be developed and decisions made. These problems usually involve many people and much money. Thus there is widespread concern with urban traffic congestion, smog, ghettos, blight, and riots; conflict of interest between suburb and central city; and sprawl, urban design, and the quality of urban life. In the past, a few economists worked in

---

6 Kenneth E. Boulding, *Economics as a Science* (New York: McGraw-Hill Book Company, 1970), p. 153.

well defined fields touching on some of the problems. Some public finance economists were interested in metropolitan finance; some real-estate economists, in general patterns of urban space use; and some transportation economists, in urban highways. After World War II, a keen general awareness of the growth of cities and the tendent economic problems began to develop. And then a creative synthesis occurred, with the formulation to the idea that these problems and efforts could be organized into an inter-related field of activity. This made sense in terms of the application of the economist's special capabilities. On a general level, the city itself is an economic entity—a social institution for economizing. In terms of particulars, the problem areas had important economic features that could be best analyzed by a professional economist. This synthesis worked, the field took hold, and in the last ten years there has been an iterative and interacting development of institutional base and intellectual content.[7]

A. Social Science and the Urban Process

The urban environment is a complex social phenomena. The social sciences, particularly sociology, political science, economics, psychology, and social anthropology, are designed (1) to analyze and bring order to the confusing multiplicity of the interacting social processes, (2) provide the base of identification of causal relationships, and (3) to bring control and predictability to the urban phenomenon. That this research must remain interdisciplinary in nature is clear. There are no purely economic considerations devoid of political, social, psychological, and administrative implications. These noneconomic factors are not usually within the skill spectrum of traditional economists. Thus economics in isolation is incapable of "shedding much light on what is to come, much less managing urban economics. Economic factors are tangled with noneconomic factors, and operational considerations beyond mere research intrude themselves into all questions."[8]

In addition to the difficulty of isolating the economic variables from the noneconomic ones, the goals of societal urban policy

---

[7] See Irving Hoch, *Progress in Urban Economics* (Washington, D. C.: Resources for the Future, 1969), p. 142.
[8] H. Wentworth Eldridge, "Introduction to Chapter 4, Urban Economics," *Taming Megatropolis* (Garden City, Doubleday and Co., 1967), p. 156.

need not necessarily be those identified by urban economists. The goal orientation of the economic discipline can be directed toward two disparate ends: (1) economic efficiency, or (2) economic effectiveness. Economic efficiency is the goal of obtaining an optimal allocation of resources—the distribution of resources such that no change in the existing allocative pattern would result in a greater value of output. Economic efficiency is simply one relative value among an array of relative values, or one social goal in a matrix of social goals. Within this matrix, social goals may be complementary to one another or they may conflict and be mutually exclusive. The importance or priority of the social goal of economic efficiency depends on the social values of the society.

Economic effectiveness requires the identification of the values that should prevail in a society so that its resources may be allocated to obtain those ends. The goal of economic efficiency is important but, in all probability, it is the goal of economic effectiveness that should prevail within the urban environment. However, social evaluation remains one of the greatest unsolved and, perhaps, unsolvable problems of our social system.[9]

What constitutes "the good city," "the good urban life," and the dynamic process within the good city? These questions econ-

---

[9] The concern that urban economics not become simply an engineering problem directed to obtain efficiency allocation of resources is reflected by Leo F. Schnore and Eric Lampard, *Social Science in the City* (New York: Frederick A. Prager, 1968), p. 24. "Serious scientific research must continue to be concerned with the fundamental questions of understanding the whole urban environment and not just those aspects which currently appear to be problems to the social engineers. And here it is a matter of appropriate emphasis rather than priorities. What does urbanization do to the growth structure and the behavior of populations in towns and countries. What forms of economic activity are most advantageously located in cities? What patterns of urban growth are most conducive to total economic growth in the light of rising population pressures? It is only when such general questions have been answered that economic and social advantages in particular places can be made. Questions about the extent to which various productive resources can be used for housing, education, health, and welfare must be tested not only against the criteria of their relative contributions to growth, but against other criteria, for example, controlling human fertility which is critical and determinative of output per capita."

omists as economists cannot answer. They must be answered ultimately through the expression of the social values of the society. Once urban goals are determined, the role of economics is to identify alternative effective uses of scarce resources to achieve these ends. The question of urban goals and priorities is, perhaps, the true dilemma of the cities. There is little agreement about what a city should be. The absence of a concensus stems from the differing value structures held within urban society. This dispersion is socially desirable. It constitutes a part of the variety and cultural variation that generate the lure of the city. But this variegated social structure creates a complex problem for setting the guidelines of social policy. These differing value premises are components in the concept of what constitutes "the good city." When one advocates a concept of what a city should be, it must be based on certain value premises. The value premises on which concepts of the good city are based must be made explicit and not held in the form of tacit assumptions.

2

The Urban Perspective:
Its History and Future

The city as a complex, dynamic social organization cannot be understood separately from the economic, social, and political forces and institutions that sustain and insure it. Another important dimension is its history—the panorama of urbanization from its inception, the forces generating and conditioning the emergence and growth of cities. A final dimension in the continuum of history is the perspective of the future—the projection of historical and present trends of urbanization into the future and the cognition of the consequences and possibilities of these changes for the urban environment and culture.

Cities have existed for approximately six thousand years. Yet for most of this time their scale and function have been diminutive compared to the contemporary metropolis and the potential urban concentration of the twenty-first century. The great cities of antiquity such as Rome, Alexandria, and Constantinople had populations of less than one million (Figure 2-1). It was the Industrial Revolution that accelerated the pace of urbanization. The division and specialization of labor made possible by advancing industrial technology necessitated the concentration of labor. The enclosure movement, by wresting people from the land, generated the necessary supply of labor and concentrated it in the cities. This process of declining rural opportunities and ur-

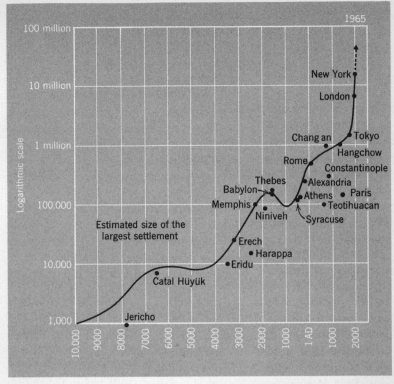

Figure 2–1. Urban size in history. (*Source. The Region's Growth, 1967,* by Regional Plan Association, Inc., New York.)

ban-centered labor markets has continued from the Industrial Revolution to the present.

The dynamics of industrial technology created the possibility of the metropolis. True urbanization is a relatively recent phenomenon. Because of the brief historical span of the United States, its cities are comparatively young. There is little historical experience to assist it in dealing with many of the problems of urban environment. This deficiency of experience is particularly acute in relation to the problems created by the aging and deteriorating physical facilities in the city.

I. URBANIZATION TRENDS: DEMOGRAPHIC, GEOGRAPHICAL, AND TECHNOLOGICAL DETERMINANTS

The pattern and nature of urban development in the United States are a product of the historical development of this country, its demographic trends, and the changing demand structure for natural resources. Urban areas were first established along the eastern seacoast. Cities such as New York, Philadelphia, Baltimore, Charleston, and Boston were components of the export base of the United States economy during the nineteenth century, or the mercantile era in economic development.[1]

In that period neither the national nor the urban economies were self-sufficient. Cities were transshipment points through which the more developed metropolitan system of Western Europe exploited domestic natural resources of the United States and distributed manufactured products to the interior. Cities were designed to service the hinderlands. Natural resource-related activities, particularly agriculture, radiated outward from the internal locus of these cities. The first available data on the population of this country, the 1790 Census, indicated that only 5% of the population was urbanized. At that time there were 24 urban places of, at least, 2500 population. New York was the largest with a population of 33,000.[2]

The early westward movement of population and economic activity were contained by natural barriers like the Appalachian Mountains. A wave theory of development and urban growth postulates that the direction and intensity of the economic development of this continent created pressures on geographical and transportation barriers, and they ultimately spilled over into the heartland of the continent. Natural accesses, technological developments and transportation modes provided increased mobility. The inland waterways system of the Appalachian area

---

[1] See Constance McLaughlin Green, *American Cities and the Growth of the Nation* (New York: Harper and Row, 1957).

[2] Helen B. Schaeffer, "Population Profile of the United States," in *Editorial Research Reports on the Urban Environment* (Washington, D. C. Congressional Quarterly, Inc., 1969), p. 12.

opened the heartland to the continued expansion and exploitation of natural resources and to the development of distant and extensive hinterlands. Cities located adjacent to rivers (Cincinnati, St. Louis, and New Orleans) developed as major transshipment and trading points. These cities developed in response to, and created a stimulus for, extensive development of the areas served by river transport.

Later, technological developments in transportation permitted further expansion and the growth of new urban centers. The canal system facilitated transportation to other areas. The development of the steamboat created more efficient and economical use of rivers and lake systems. The railroads aided a process of growth unparalleled in United States history, providing efficient transportation throughout the Midwest and Southwest, and later to the West. Railroads reinforced expansion of urban areas such as Cincinnati and St. Louis, and created new centers (Chicago) as gateways to massive agricultural resources.

. . . No Community in America illustrates the effects of this new form of transport so well as Chicago. Using the railroads as a means of tying the vast hinterlands securely to her own interest, she showed other cities how an urban empire could develop. Her newspapers, her innovating methods of marketing and her infectious belief in her own significance in national affairs long gave her a unique position in the United States. She came to symbolize the vitality, the vulgarity, and the violence of urban America. But her strength was impressive. Few Americans needed further proof of the benefits the railroads would bring. Mining towns in the mountains, agricultural villages in the plains, and settlements in the forests of the far northwest all saw in railroads their hope for the future.[3]

As fuller exploitation of the inland waterways and the development of railroading created new markets and sources of raw materials, the New England economy was transformed from purely export orientation to industrialization. From New England, the industrialization of large urban areas moved westward to new locations that were closer to the sources of raw materials and had easier access to markets. Many cities in the Midwest

---

[3] Constance McLaughlin Green, *American Cities and the Growth of the Nation,* op. cit., p. 244.

(including the river cities and Chicago) developed processing industries during the initial stages of industrialization.

The result of ongoing processes—population growth, industrialization and declining rural opportunities—was the urbanization of the nation. By 1920 the United States had become a predominately urban country; 51.2% of its residents lived in urban places. The percentage of the total population living in rural areas declined throughout the nineteenth century and during the initial half of the twentieth. By 1960 the absolute number of rural inhabitants also had declined and the rural population constituted only 30% of the total population. In 1965 two-thirds of the population was urbanized in the existing 219 standard metropolitan areas.[4]

Throughout the process of rapid growth and development, the forces of industrialization and urbanization have been dependent on the supply of natural resources relative to the changing demand structure for these resources. "In the agricultural period the most valued natural endowment was arable land with environmental components of climate and water. During industrialization, a new set of mineral resources became important. In the 20th century, service activities and amenity resources have exerted an increasingly strong pull on industry and in people."[5]

The post-1950 growth of the various regions has been associated with the growth of the service sector; the increase in the number of footloose industries, such as aircraft, aerospace, defense industries, and research and development; the expansion and interregional migration of the non-job oriented population; and the overall rising real incomes. As a result of these developments, new amenity resources have moved to the forefront of the national economy. New advantages for economic growth have been found around the "outer rim" of the country, in regions and places relatively well endowed with such amenities. Advantages have been cumulative, for the regional growth within the context of the national pattern of heart-

---

[4] Helen B. Schaeffer, "Population Profile of the United States," op. cit., p. 12.

[5] Brian J. L. Barry and Elaine Neils, "Location, Size, and Shape of Cities as Influenced by Environmental Factors: The Urban Environment Writ Large," in Harvey S. Perloff, *The Quality of the Urban Environment* (Baltimore: Johns Hopkins Press, 1969), p. 258.

land and hinterland has brought these regions to the threshold sizes for internal production of a wide variety of goods and services at the very time that changes in the definition of urban resources made rapid advance possible. Hence the explosion of metropolitan growth of the south, southwest, and west.[6]

An additional technological factor that has freed urban development from the need to be closely located to natural resources and from transportation dependence is the development of rapid communication via electronic data. The exchange of ideas, information, and expertise is becoming a major component of the service sector. Thus, increasingly, cities perform and function as a communications system or as "idea interchanges."[7] Technological developments indicate that we will be able to make intellectual expertise equally available throughout the country. If information and ideas become ubiquitous, there will no longer be a single best place for management activity. Every place will become as good a location as every other.[8]

At one time cities were primarily places to trade; the places which were in the best location for collecting and distributing commodities prospered and became the most important. Later, cities became places to produce goods, and those with access to raw materials and markets for their products became dominant. Today large cities are the best places to produce ideas, and locations in which information and ideas are most abundant are most important. Tomorrow, information activities, management and education will continue to be important, but tele-communications will free us—if we wish to be freed—from the high density metropolitan existence we now find necessary. We are, for the first time in the histories of cities, in a position to assure that the best places to live become our most important cities.[9]

II. FUTURE URBANIZATION TRENDS

Future urbanization trends and rates will be influenced by many variables including changing social and cultural attitudes toward life styles and the rate of demographic growth in the

---

[6] Op. cit., pp. 265–267.
[7] Ron Febler, "What Makes Cities Important," *Bell Telephone Magazine*, March/April 1970, p. 12.
[8] Op. cit., p. 15.
[9] *Ibid.*

United States. However, if past trends provide an adequate base for projections, urbanization is only in its incipient phases.

The predominant factor influencing the growth of urban areas is a population increase. Demographers have provided four different projections of population growth that are based on differing assumptions about fertility rates. If these projections are realized, the population will be between 255 and 300 million persons in 1990. If the decline in the number of persons living in rural areas and the percentage increase in the number of persons living in urban areas continues at historical rates, the majority of this population increase will be in urban environments. This projection is based on the assumption that our cities will continue to be inhabitable and that the critical urban problems such as rising crime rates and declining environmental quality can be reversed.

Projections of urbanization of the population based on the assumption that the city continues to be habitable indicate that the urbanized population will increase approximately 137% or in excess of 135 million persons in urbanized areas by the year 2000 (see table 2-1). The period 1940 to 1960 witnessed an increase of 130% in the total urbanized land area in the United States, which was attributable in part to the uneconomical use of open space within cities and the uncontained sprawl of suburbanization. Projections indicate that this rate of land consumption will decrease with a total increase in urbanized land

TABLE 2-1. Population and Land Area in Urbanized Areas of United States, Years 1920 to 2000 (*Thousands*)

	Population Total Urbanized	Percent Increase in Total Urbanized Population	Total Urbanized Land Area (Sq. Mi)	Percent Increase in Total Urbanized Land Area	Density per Square Mile
1920	38,896		6,318		6,160
1940	58,138	49.5	10,452	65.4	5,560
1960	98,680	69.7	24,111	130.68	4,090
1980	158,230	60.3	42,672	77.0	3,708
2000	234,046	48.0	65,840	54.3	3,555

Source. Homer Hoyt, "Urban Land Use Requirements," Research Monograph no. 1, Homer Hoyt Institute, Washington, D.C., 1968, p. 180.

of 173% between 1960 and 2000. The projected rate of increase in the consumption of urbanized land is greater than the rate of increase in the population of urban areas in the decades to the year 2000. As a concomitant result of this land use, the density of urbanized regions must decrease. The density of urbanized areas has been decreasing throughout the twentieth century. In 1920 there were approximately 6160 persons per square mile. By the year 2000 the proximity of persons is projected to fall to 3555 persons per square mile on the average. This is a decrease of 42.2% between 1920 and the year 2000.

III. THE FUTURE OF URBANIZATION: MEGALOPOLIS

As the size of cities increases, at some point they may become contiguous to one another resulting in an interlocking chain of extensive urban complexes, or "megalopolis." These large urban regions may well be the form of urbanization in the future. However it should be noticed that these projections "presume the maintenance of a basically laissez-faire role by government and industry with respect to future growth patterns."[10]

Megalopolis, however, does exist in a "continuous corridor of urbanization on the Atlantic seaboard stretching from southern New Hampshire to northern Virginia and from the Atlantic to the Appalachian foothills."

No other section of the United States has such a large concentration of population, with such a high average density, spread over such a large area. And no other section has a comparable role within the nation or a comparable importance in the world. Here has been developed a kind of supremacy, in politics, in economics, and possibly even in cultural activities, seldom before attained by an area of this size.[11]

More than thirty-eight million people live in megalopolis. It contains five of the fifteen largest cities in the United State: Boston, New York,

10 Advisory Commission on Intergovernmental Relations, *Urban and Rural America: Policies for Future Growth* (Washington, D. C.: United States Government Printing Office, 1968), p. 14.
11 Jean Gottmann in *Megalopolis: The Urbanized Northeastern Seaboard of the United States* (New York: Twentieth Century Fund, 1961), p. 3.

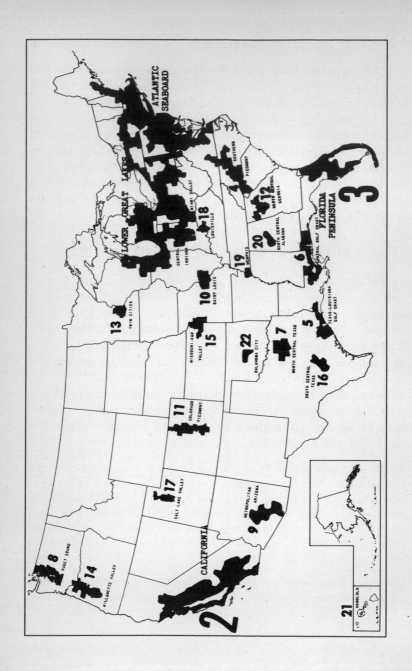

Figure 2-2. Urban Regions in the year 2000. This map shows 22 United States urban regions projected to have a population of one million or more 30 years from now. In the year 2000, the Atlantic Seaboard Urban Region has merged with the Lower Great Lakes Urban Region to form a single Metropolitan Belt containing more than 126 million people. Two other major urban regions have spread in California and Florida.

The urban regions now are growing as if national frontiers did not exist. Detroit's air pollution already engulfs Windsor, Ontario. The Lower Great Lakes Urban Region has its Canadian counterpart—a Canadian Urban Region that now extends from Windsor to Buffalo and Oshawa, and is projected to spread until it links up with a series of cities and metropolitan regions going beyond Montreal to the Trois Rivieres metropolitan complex.

This unprecedented Great North American Urban Region is projected to contain over a third of the Canadian population and 41% of the United States population.

On the Pacific Coast, the Puget Sound Urban Region is merging with Canada's Fraser River Valley region and may eventually include Vancouver, Seattle, and Tacoma in one region. The Southern California Urban Region, meanwhile, extends into Mexico south of San Diego.

Note: Urban regions must have, at least, one million population to qualify. This projection was made while Pickard was director of the Program Analysis and Evaluation Staff at the United States Department of Housing and Urban Development.

Figure 2-2

Population of Future Urban Regions of the United States

	Population in Millions	
	1970 (estimated)	2000 (projected)
1. Metropolitan Belt	86.2	126.5
Atlantic Seaboard	45.8	67.4
Lower Great Lakes	40.4	59.1
2. California	19.9	42.5
3. Peninsular Florida	5.7	13.0
4. Southern Peidmont	3.3	5.2
5. Texas-Louisiana Gulf Coast	2.5	4.9
6. Central Gulf Coast	2.7	4.7
7. North Central Texas	2.2	4.2
8. Puget Sound	2.1	3.8
9. Metropolitan Arizona	1.3	3.5
10. Saint Louis	2.4	3.5
11. Colorado Piedmont	1.6	3.2
12. North Central Georgia	1.8	3.1
13. Twin Cities	1.8	2.5
14. Willamet Valley	1.4	2.4
15. Missouri-Kaw Valley	1.5	2.3
16. South Central Texas	1.2	2.2
17. Salt Lake Valley	0.8	1.6
18. Louisville	0.9	1.5
19. Memphis	0.8	1.4
20. North Central Alabama	0.8	1.3
21. Honolulu (Oahu)	0.7	1.2
22. Oklahoma City	0.6	1.2
Total (U.S.)	142.2	235.7
% of total U.S. population in urban regions	69.3%	76.8%

Philadelphia, Baltimore and Washington. But megalopolis is not a nightmare extension of Times Square. The region is not only the financial, business, and governmental hub of the nation; it is also a large manufacturing region, and it produces substantial quantities of agricultural products. The population of megalopolis is, on the average, the richest, best educated, best housed and best serviced group of its size in the world. The area's boundaries are expected in time to push into Maine and reach down into southern Virginia.[12]

Jean Gottmann, who has documented the growth and function of megalopolis, argues that technology and population growth will create new dimensions and new opportunities for urbanization in the future. The urban area will take new forms—a structure implied or observable throughout megalopolis.

This region serves thus as a laboratory in which we may study the new evolutionary shape of both the meaning of our traditional vocabulary and the whole material structure of our way of life . . . . So great are the consequences of the general evolution heralded by the present rise in complexity of megalopolis that analysis of this region's problems often gives one the feeling of looking at the dawn of a new stage in human civilization . . . . Indeed the area may be considered the cradle of a new order of the organization of inhabited space.[13]

It is projected that four great urban centers will assimilate the major portions of the increase in urban population between 1970 and the year 2000 (see Figure 2-2, page 20). By the year 2000 these four centers will contain approximately 187 million persons or 60% of the population of the nation. These regions are as follows.[14] (1) A five-hundred mile corridor containing 67.9 million people along the Atlantic seaboard, stretching from Boston to Washington, D.C. (2) A chain of cities extending nearly 1000 miles from Utica, New York, west to Chicago and north along the western shore of Lake Michigan to Green Bay, Wisconsin,

---

[12] Jeanne Kuebler, "Megalopolis: Promise and Problems" in *Editorial Research Reports on the Urban Environment,* op. cit., pp. 26–27.
[13] Jean Gottmann, op. cit., p. 9.
[14] This information is drawn from the Advisory Commission on Intergovernmental Relations, *Urban and Rural America: Policies for Future Growth,* op. cit., p. 14. They were originally presented in Jerome P. Pickard, *Dimensions of Metropolitanism,* Urban Land Institute Research Monograph 14 (Washington, D.C.: 1967), p. 23.

which will contain 60.8 million people. This will be linked with the east coast megalopolis forming a super-megalopolis of 128.7 million people. (3) On the Pacific coast there will be an urban belt of 500 miles between San Francisco through Los Angeles to San Diego which will contain approximately 44.5 million people. (4) A metropolitan complex will stretch 350 miles along the Atlantic coast between Jacksonville and Miami, Florida and move westward across the Florida peninsula to the Tampa—St. Petersburg metropolitan area and will ultimately contain 13.8 million persons. Other urban regions of lesser size will contain an additional 52 million people. Thus 241 million persons or 77% of the population occupying approximately 11% of the nation's land will be concentrated in urban regions.

IV. THE INTERNATIONAL MEGALOPOLIS[15]

If the projections of megalopian growth are realized, its logical conclusion will be the extension of socially, economically and, perhaps, politically interrelated urban continuums crossing international boundaries. Constantinos Doxiadis, noted Greek city planner, is engaged in an ongoing and continually updated project of estimating what the urbanized world will look like a century from now—the nature and form of the labyrinth of crisscrossing bands of urbanization across continents (see Figure 2-3). He has designated this ultimate stage of urbanization as the universal city, or "ecumenic city," or "Ecumenopolis." Although projections of this nature must remain tentative and problematical, the conclusions derived from this process are intriguing and of significant import to the urbanologist.

They are made on the basis of the forces that are currently at work shaping the nature and direction of the urban process.[16]

1. *Population.* The world now is in a population explosion phase. It is expected to last from 100 to 150 years, and reach from 20 to 30 billion people. Then it will show a marked slow-

---

15 Mason Wade, Editor, *The International Megalopolis,* Toronto: University of Toronto Press, 1969.
16 *Christian Science Monitor,* September 9, 1968, p. C-1.

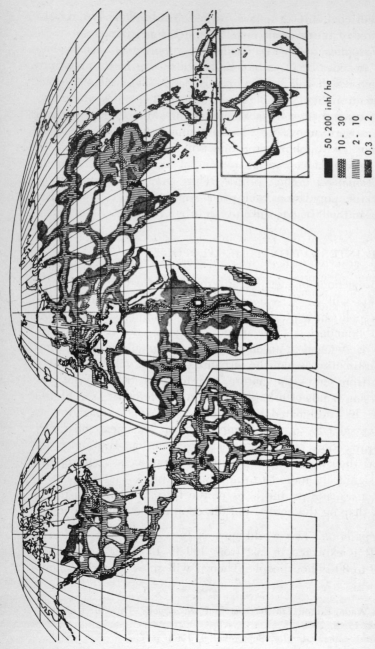

Figure 2–3. Ecumenopolis at the end of the twenty-first century. This map, based on studies by the Athens Center of Ekistics, suggests the urban pattern in the year 2100, when the world is presumed to have 20 to 30 billion people. (*Source. The Futurist,* October 1970, p. 169.)

50 - 200 inh/ha
10 - 30
2 - 10
0.3 - 2

down period. This slowdown will coincide with the relative saturation of economically inhabitable living space.

2. *Habitable area.* Taking climate, topography, and technological improvements into consideration, the earth may have from 15 to 25 million square miles of habitable space 100 to 150 years in the future.

3. *Maximum population.* It will be possible for the earth to sustain a maximum population of around 50 billion, from the standpoint of water, food, production, energy output, and environmental balance.

4. *Technology.* The technology of communications, transportation, energy production, private control, and public utilities will shape the "City of the Future."

On the basis of the projections, Doxiadis concludes:

We will be, therefore, faced with a universal city huge in proportions in relation to the present one, with many more people, much greater numbers of machines, but with far greater economic forces and technological and scientific knowledge. This is the city of the future with which we will have to deal. This is the city that may be the ultimate phase of urban development on our earth, or at least the next phase at which humanity will stop for many generations, many centuries, or many thousands of years to come. It may live as long as the small cities of the past have lived—or almost 6000 to 7000 years —by which time humanity may enter a new phase of its evolution and develop something which is completely inconceivable today.[17]

All scholars do not observe the rise in megalopolis with the same enthusiasm as Jean Gottman or the equanimity of Constantinos Doxiadis. Lewis Mumford, the noted observer of the urban milieu believes that cities have life cycles with three stages of ascension and three stages of decline, with Megalopolis being the first stage of the decline. The stages Mumford identifies are:[18]

Stage 1, *Eopolis—the rise of the village community.* This is the

---

17 Constantinos A. Doxiadis, "How to Build A City of the Future," and Richard Eells, and Clarence Walton, Editors, *Man and the City of the Future* (London: Collier-McMillian Limited, 1968), p. 178.
18 Lewis Mumford, *The Culture of Cities* (New York: Harcourt, Brace & World, Inc., 1938), pp. 284–292.

incipient phase of urbanization when man first began to centralize his mutual activities into permanent habitations and institutions of association. This possibility of association is predicated
on the extensive development of agriculture and the domestica-
tion of animals. Mumford argues that this village community is
the prototype of the city and "its life underlies all subsequent
transformations of civilization."[19]

Stage 2, Polis. As mutual needs are realized between villages
or centralized groups, they tend to associate to attain these common ends. Specifically, these ends are the need of defense against
predators and deprivation, the common need of religious communities, the rise of a systematic division of labor, and the early
stages of specializations of functions in trades, crafts, and
mechanization. In addition, for the first time, the phenomenon
of leisure time begins to arise, releasing men for those pursuits
that are productive of learning and culture.

Stage 3, Metropolis. As one city gains ascendency within its
region and differentiates itself from other towns and villages,
it becomes the mother city or focal point within the hierarchy of
towns based on some comparative advantage. Trade begins on
an extensive scale with other regions. During this stage, there
is more extensive and complete specialization of economic, social,
and institutional functions. The administrative skills necessary
to coordinate the institutions of the city are developed, and the
centralized administration occurs. The extensions of the cultural heritage characterized by the city continues and reaches
its zenith in this stage.

However, Mumford argues that signs of weakness begin to
appear beneath the surface. He feels that there is "increasing
failure to absorb and integrate disparate cultural elements: the
beginnings of individualism that tends to disrupt all social bonds
without creating a new order on a higher plane."[20]

Stage 4, Megalopolis. This is the beginning of the decline.
The decline of the city is conceptualized by Mumford in terms
of the deterioration of the urban culture that was the raison
d'etre and the highest achievement of the city. "The moral sense

---

[19] Ibid., p. 285.
[20] Ibid., p. 289.

becomes more callous and the will to culture increasingly important."[21] Persons begin to turn from those things that create culture and civilization to the pursuit of the aggrandisement of wealth and to the ostentatious display of physical things. Bigness and standardization as social ends become dominant. Energy is diverted from biological and social ends to the creation of physical goods. "The city as a means of association, as a haven of culture, becomes a means of disassociation and a growing threat to real culture."[22]

Stage 5, Tyrannopolis. Parasitism comes to characterize the city. The culture continues to deteriorate with continuing emphasis on display and expense. The political and economic institutional framework of the city begins to deteriorate with the widespread moral apathy and failure of civic responsibility. Life becomes demoralized, uncertainty hangs over every prospect of the future. There is municipal and state bankruptcy, and productive work in the arts and sciences ceases. The beginnings of an exodus from the Megalopolis occurs.

Stage 6, Nekropolis. This is the final stage in the urban continuum. Mumford's description of the apocalypse of the city is foreboding.

. . . famine and disease wrack both the countryside and the city. The physical towns become mere shells. Those remaining there are unable to carry on the old municipal services or to maintain the old civic life. What remains of that life is at best a clumsy caricature. The names persist; the reality vanishes. Monuments and books no longer convey meaning: the old routine of life involves too much effort to carry on: . . . relapse into the more primitive and rural occupation . . . the living forms of the ancient city become a tune for dying. Sand sweeps over the ruins, the soul of Babylon, Nineveh, Rome. In short, Nekropolis, the city of the dead: flesh turned into ashes, life turned into a meaningless pillar of salt.[23]

In later writings, Mumford has countered those sociologists and economists who base their predictions on a linear or curvilinear extrapolation of forces currently at work. "Under the

---

21 Ibid., p. 289.
22 Ibid., p. 290.
23 Ibid., pp. 291–292.

guise of objective statistical description, these social scientists are in fact leaving out of their analysis, the observable data of biology, anthropology or history that would destroy their premises or rectify their conclusions."[24]

The criticism of these projections are placed within the context of an ecological framework. Mumford argues that these statisticians possess only a superficial regard for life and health and possess either a lack of knowledge or a deep contempt for "organic processes that involve maintaining the complex function of all organic forms, in an environment favorable to life in all its manifestations."[25] Thus he contends that there are ecological limitations to the growth of the city that will cause the megalopolis to be a highly unstable social system with disintegration and decay parameters created by the limits of the city as an organic and biological entity.

These crisis dimensions of the urban environment are not new to the city. European cities have faced the question of growth, decay, and renewal throughout the century. However, many of these problems are just becoming apparent in cities in the United States because of their relative youth and the dynamic performance of the economy throughout most of the twentieth century. All of these problems have historical antecedents and future ramifications for the ongoing vitality of the city. Thus it is important that the historical context and future projections of the city be a part of the perspective that the student of the urban environment includes in his study of the city.

---

[24] Lewis Mumford, *The City and History; Its Work, Its Transformations, and Its Prospects,* Harcourt Brace & World, Inc. (New York: 1961), p. 527.
[25] Ibid.

3

The Structure of Economic
Activity in Urban Areas

I. FORMS OF DESCRIPTION OF URBAN ECONOMIES

Most urban economies can be characterized by cliches that reflect geographical, social, and economic characteristics of the city. Terms such as "Fun City," the "Queen City," are typical nonfunctional descriptions. Other descriptions such as the "Pork Capital of the World," "the Stock Market Center," "the Automotive City," are functionally oriented and have quasi-economic implications. These impressionistic caricatures of urban economies refer to the type of output or places where residents work, or describe a basic manufacturing emphasis or other activity.

More functional descriptions of urban economies, like those that appear in the following illustrations, indicate the type of industries and services, the composition of output, and the dominance of particularly advantageous economic endowment.

1. Cleveland has excellent transportation facilities, and cheap and adequate supplies of industrial energy.

2. Boston, which faced competitive disadvantage in most traditional manufacturing, has developed industries that utilize skilled labor and professionally trained technicians.

3. Urban areas found principally in the West have little intercity competition and dominate and serve large surrounding areas. Kansas City, for example, is the only large urban area

within a 200-mile radius and is the major financial center for the Midwest.

4. Dallas is a service center with no specialization in particular manufacturing.

5. Denver is an example of a regional center that is the major commercial and financial city in the Mountain States.

6. Minneapolis-St. Paul is located favorably in terms of agriculture as well as manufacturing. This area has developed the distribution and processing of agricultural products grown in the Great Plains as well as manufacturing products.

7. In the analysis of employment by industry sectors in Harlem, data indicate that Harlem does not have the infrastructure and financial activities that characterize the city of New York.

Its disproportionately larger retail sector is inadequately supported by a wholesaling base—a base less than one-third of the relative size of this activity in similar areas throughout the city. This activity mix cannot be explained simply by referring to the area as a residential neighborhood. Harlem's economic development has been a process whereby mixed industrial-residential neighborhood has deteriorated through the inability of its residents to command the resources necessary to implement a balance type of growth. Businessmen have established themselves in the retail market because they are excluded from entry into more capital-intensive wholesale and more infrastructural support activities.[1]

The Harlem example confirms the uneven distribution of economic vitality in the New York City area.

8. The comparative growth rate of employment in New York City and its suburbs reflects continuing industrial decentralization and increasing employment opportunities in office-related jobs. The New York City employment base has never been dominated by mass production industrial plants as is the case in older industrial centers such as Chicago, Pittsburgh, and Detroit. "Manufacturing in New York has been largely made up of industries able to accommodate to multi-level loft build-

---

[1] T. Vietorisz and B. Harrison, *Economic Development of Harlem,* New York: Praeger Publishers, 1970, p. 34; also see O. D. Duncan, *Metropolis and Region,* Baltimore: Johns Hopkins Press, 1960, p. 136ff.

ings, street congestion, and all other attributes of central locations."[2]

The dynamics of urban change cause both development and vitality of decline and "depression." The depressed terminology may be applied to new urban centers or to mature areas. A depressed urban area has substantial and persistent unemployment, low median family income, high out-migration, and prospects for sudden downturns in the employment rate.

9. Pittsburgh is an example of a mature depressed area. Despite a slightly above average per capita income, Pittsburgh has a very slow growth rate. The basic cause of the long-term change in the economic environment is the decline of employment in the steel industry as a whole. With dependence on steel, when steel demand slackens, the Pittsburgh area immediately reflects the decline, and unemployment rises rapidly.

10. An example of a rapidly growing area with depressed characteristics is Los Angeles. Although per capita income is very high and economic growth seems rapid, the rate of unemployment is also very high. High unemployment in the region is a function of the relationship between the rate of in-migration and job opportunities. The relationship is important and interesting because in-migration, or increased population, in and of itself is not advantageous to the economy of every urban area. The problem in Los Angeles is a function of the slowdown in the rate of development of defense-related manufacturing. Although employment in defense-related industries grew at a rapid rate during the 1960s, structural shifts in defense needs resulted in a reduction in demand for the output of the area's defense industries. Employment is declining, but the in-migration continues.

II. DETERMINANTS OF INCOME AND EMPLOYMENT

The essential and important economic characteristic of any urban area is the level of employment, production, and income. In macroeconomics, expenditures or spending determines the

---

[2] Dick Netzer, "New York's Mixed Economy: Ten Years Later," *The Public Interest*, No. 16, Summer 1969, p. 191.

level of employment and income. There are only three participating economic expenditure units in urban areas: (a) the private consumers who buy local or nonlocally produced goods and services of durable and nondurable type; (b) business units that buy local or external resources in the form of capital outlays, raw material, and employ labor for the processing or production of semifinished or finished goods; and (c) the public sector which includes agencies of the federal, state, county, and the municipal government, and various other local political units (for example, sewer, lighting, or irrigation districts within the urban geographical boundaries). Each governmental unit taxes, transfers money, and purchases resources. In addition, the urban economy also has a "foreign sector." Goods and services are exported to buyers outside the city, and are imported by buyers from outside areas into the local markets.

III. MONEY FLOWS AMONG URBAN SPENDING UNITS

The flow of money between the various spending units is illustrated in Figure 3-1. Households earn income from private sector businesses and the local government and spend the money for purchases of private and public goods and services and, of course, save and pay city taxes. Business receipts come from purchases by local households, and from sales of goods and services outside the city. Businesses pay local and nonlocal taxes and purchase goods and services and resources inside and outside of the city. Nonlocal tax payments and the purchases of resources outside the city by households and businesses are losses or leakages from the urban economy. Household earnings from outside the city add to local income flows. The city government is a purchaser of local goods and services and is an importer. City government leakages from the local economy are in the form of purchases of goods and resources from nonlocal governments and nonlocal businesses, and in the form of the transfer of city revenues to other nonlocal governments.

Stated in another way, consumption, plus business investment and housing investment, in addition to local government investment and the purchases of goods and services, are the income determinants in the urban economy. The urban "foreign sector"

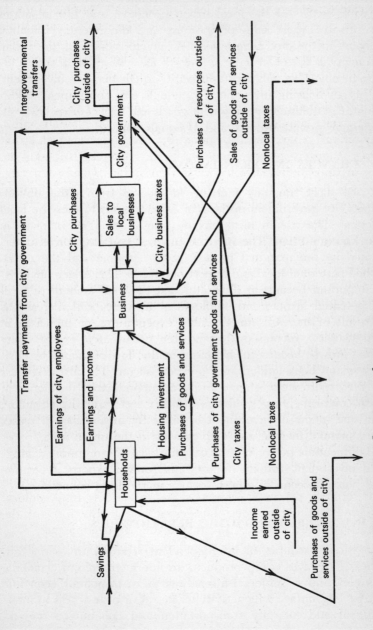

Figure 3–1. Illustrative money flows in an urban economy.

33

must be included as an income determinant. The "foreign sector" includes the leakages of imports consumed by the public and private sectors of the local urban economy, and the injections of private export sales of business and the intergovernmental income to the city government. A "macro model" of the urban economy is $Y_n = C + I_b + I_h + I_m + P_m + X_c - M$. Y equals urban income, C equals consumption, I_b equals business investment, I_h equals housing investment, I_m equals city government investment, P_m equals city government goods and services expenditures, X_c equals private exports, and M equals imports.

IV. CHANGES IN URBAN INCOME

In the short run, any increase in income from either investment, city government outlays, or exports tends to increase local income. The rise in local income brings about an increase in local consumption. The increase in local consumption is determined by the marginal propensity to consume and the established pattern of local and import purchases. This "macroanalysis" is important because it illustrates that the total amount or level of potential income and employment in a city will increase as a result of increases in available expenditures or increases in productivity. Increased demand for urban area exports may bring growth because of increases in the flow of money to businesses and householders in the export sector. The attractiveness of the export sector should bring about industrial development with complementary spillovers in other sectors of the economy. Any net inflow of investment or labor for any reason increases the potential income and employment in the urban area.

Differentials between nonlocal and local consumption, savings and investment, foreign imports and foreign exports determine the potential economic performance in the local economy.

V. INTER-URBAN ECONOMIC RELATIONSHIPS

Large cities exhibit an interdependent relationship to one another. This relationship produces an intermetropolitan economic complex and a subject for analysis of metropolitan economic activity. Manufacturing activity locates at or near access to interregional and intercity transportation and communication. and close to large sales or market areas. Manufacturing activity locates in and around metropolitan areas as a function of the distance to the nearest metropolitan market area. Population density is an indicator of the limits of economic activity in a given metropolitan area. High population density is consistent with a high level of manufacturing and related activity, and reflects the fact that urban manufacturing locations are oriented toward accessibility of final product marketing areas rather than of source or supply of inputs or raw materials. In terms of the historical growth of cities, extractive industries seem to decrease relatively as city population increases, while manufacturing and fabricating industries grow with the increasing size of cities. The pattern of local and nonlocal services is proportionally related to the growth in the size of the city (see Table 4-2).

The development of selected industries in an urban economy increase or decrease the urban economy's exports of expenditures and resources or imports of finished products, money, and other resources. For any community to grow, the city must have a flow of new money, or increasing exports. In a given urban economy, if the flow of export monies declines or simply does not increase, the local economy will not grow and may become a depressed urban area. The export sales effect on urban areas will vary with the economic characteristics of a given city or with the type of industry, the location, the size of the market, specialization, the integration of industries, the income of residents, the pattern of consumption, and the stage of growth of the urban economy.

Regardless of the industrial base, urban areas are characterized by unique specialization. With specialization, there is economic interdependence within and without the city. Urban economies in the United States have a commanding necessity to trade with other urban areas because of specialization. The export of products and services, from a given urban area, provides the means by which a city can grow. Interdependence between producing areas is important (see Table 4-3).

VI. EXPORT AND IMPORT MULTIPLIER CONCEPTS

The type of industrial structure that is desirable in an urban economy can, in part, be evaluated in terms of the impact of purchases and expenditures of its industries on the local economy.

Business investment and the related multiplier generate aggregate spending determined by the multiplier factor multiplied by the increments of investment

$$I \times \frac{1}{1 - mpc}$$

The injections of new money into local economy may or may not be retained in the local economy because of the economy's role in either the region or in the national economy. The critical variables in expansion through the investment multiplier are the volume of exports from the local economy and the levels of local investment.

A change in exports in the local urban economy results in a change in local income by some multiple of the dollar value of the exports. An export multiplier will determine the amount or that change in local income. No local economy is closed. With the absence of the tariff-type trade barriers, the local economy is in a "free trade" environment. The concept of the export multiplier is basically the same as the investment multiplier but the injections are eroded by the pattern of spending of the local marginal propensity to consume, and the marginal propensity to import. The *MPI* is the measure of the incremental propensities to buy nonlocally produced goods. The larger the marginal propensity to the import, the smaller the change in local income will be. The smaller the marginal propensity to import, the larger the incremental changes in local aggregate demand will be. In a formula relationship the local economy multiplier equals 1/1-(*mpc-mpi*). Thus a city with an industrial base that provides for a high level of export goods and that also provides residences with ample shopping opportunities for goods and services is likely to have a lower marginal propensity to import than a city that is a service-industry locale or does not have outlets for locally produced goods.

In the analysis of the growth pattern of local economies, the export activity becomes a significant factor in the manner by which the local economy is able to sustain employment, or in identifying potential problems that may arise because of dependence on the economies of cities outside the local area. The size of the marginal propensity to import is important. The size is a function of the opportunities for the purchase of the goods and services provided by local business industry. Since export demand is externally determined, industries that are export dependent will show short-run variations in their level of employment and income generation as a function of conditions that occur in other economies. In a "one industry" city, whether it be the production of automobiles or whiskeys, the absence of a diversified base in the export sector has great significance in the city's short-run employment and income-generation capacities.

VII. INVESTMENT IN URBAN DEVELOPMENT

Investment expenditures in a national economy are affected by a multiplier that produces larger changes in the national income than the initial change in the level of investment outlays.

New expenditure money in the total economy produces impacts that cause patterns of expenditures which bring future growth or, perhaps, decline in the total national economy. But in an urban environment the multiplier from increased investment or other spending may or may not affect the local economy. The investment impact from a specific urban area may or may not be significant in the "outside" world. Expenditures, or the injection of increases in new money in an economy, may increase total economic activity by more or less than initial expenditures. Because the urban economy is in a national common market with no restriction on the flow of resources between and within the urban areas, the money expenditures may be exported from the community. Thus the total level of economic activity within the community may not be increased because of increases in expenditures.

Business expansion in macroeconomic terms occurs when private business decision makers invest in additional productive capacity, install new machinery, or construct new factories or office buildings after evaluating a tradeoff between cost and revenue or on profit maximization strategies. Investment will occur only when decision makers assume that the expansion of productive facilities will increase profits or returns from their business activity. Any enterpriser or business manager interested in increasing or, perhaps, in maximizing profits will invest if the return will be greater than the cost of borrowing capital or other costs associated with the expansion in capacity. Business investment decisions are made under conditions of uncertainty, since the business-decision maker must embark on a process of discounting future revenue from an investment.[3]

Assuming that there is a rational calculation of the future return of investment decisions, regardless of the method of calculation, increases in investment are also affected by factors that exert other positive and negative effects on the capacity of a business firm to sell his products effectively in the marketing sense and/or to organize resources for production at appropriate costs.

Other independent forces exert effects on investment demand in a given urban area. One of the nonincome factors is population change or population growth in an urban area. Over time, an increase in population should increase the demand for money in the local and national capital markets because of increasing consumer purchases by a larger number of people. Increases in the size of the available labor force should also increase demand for money. Technological innovations in the form of new product development or improvement in the production processes will aid in maintaining high levels of demand for capital. Technological innovation, both in construction and production, help to sustain growth, particularly, in modern industries.

An urban area that has a static population and a relatively slow incidence of technological change may reflect weak effective demand for investment capital. Investment outlays in any given area are significant as additions to the local income stream as one of the principal spending units. Investment also creates additional employment opportunities that increase the volume of goods and/or services available.

VIII. INDUSTRIAL DEVELOPMENT—THE PUBLIC SECTOR ROLE

Most urban areas have institutionalized a form of information and education as an adjunct to investment decisions. An urban government or service organization (chambers of commerce, in-

---

[3] See Warren L. Smith, *Macro Economics* (Homewood, Illinois: Richard D. Irwin, Inc., 1970), p. 168.

dustrial development offices, or the urban planning center) provide potential investors with the information necessary to determine sources of costs and benefits in the local economy. For example, the city of Phoenix advertises in a variety of trade magazines and newspapers that it has excellent support capabilities to improve the profitability of business.

Phoenix is America's fastest growing manufacturing center for science-oriented industries. You will find growth-stimulating tax structures, untapped labor pools, and diversified support facilities. Add to that a culture/academic climate in year-round sunshine. And no wonder, companies, top executives, and skilled talent find Phoenix the ideal growth and profit environment.[4]

Additional details on the advantages or the benefit sources of making a business investment in Phoenix are available from the Economic Development Department of the Chamber of Commerce in the city of Phoenix.

The typical urban industrial development office provides information on the factors that businessmen know are important in considering investment or location in plants. The list of items includes: nature of the local markets, the availability of resources, including labor, land, and buildings, plus transportation, utilities, including fuel, construction costs, community services, municipal government, public attitude, taxes, and climate. All of these factors influence in company decisions to invest in a given urban area.

IX. COMPENSATORY ACTIVITY OF LOCAL GOVERNMENTS

The national government acts as a compensatory spending unit to reduce or to expand the total volume of aggregate expenditures. Through appropriate increases or decreases in taxes and/or expenditure, the national government can reduce or increase the amount of effective aggregate demand. These fiscal policy actions are designed to be consistent with the broad economic objectives of maintaining high levels of employment and appropriate rates of economic growth.

---

4 *The Wall Street Journal,* Wednesday, January 6, 1971, p. 5.

Since city governments are political creatures of the state government, they have limited fiscal capacity to create a pro- or counter-cyclical impact on local spending. Tax sources are assigned and regulated by the state government. The level of spending of municipal governments is limited to revenue collected and by the established levels and standards of deficits.

The volume of expenditures for municipalities is determined by local demands for public services. Details concerning the generation of the supply and demand for municipal services are given in a later chapter, but it is important to observe that the capacity of municipal governments to adjust expenditures or revenues consistent with broader economic goals is virtually nonexistent.

There is little reason why a system should be created to permit city governments to act as a pro- or countercyclical agent. The impact of local spending is neutralized in direct proportion to the interrelatedness between a given urban area and other urban centers in the national market. Governments invest public funds in industrial development projects in response to the demand for potential economic benefits by the citizens in the area. The extent to which city governments subsidize industry is determined by the demand of the public citizens.

Competition for new plants and new industrial activity in urban areas is now a national competitive game. Local businessmen, public utilities, and banks invest their time and money in industrial development of an urban area with the expectations of indirect return from improved community well-being, growth, and increased spending. But industries make geographical and site selections on the basis of fundamental economic inducements and not on the basis of community promotion. Such advantageous features as low-cost loans, the provision of utility services, the financing of plant construction, or the financing of other forms of economic development aids may be marginal, but critical factors that induce a particular businessman to locate in one urban area instead of another. The extent to which the municipal government can participate in expanding the economic base of the community is limited by state constitution and statutes, the local expenditure and revenue pattern, and by the localized nature of the municipal services.

The residual role of the municipal government in industrial

growth activity is participation in the design of programs or processes to attract industry. This industrial attraction responsibility is a substitute for the role of government as an expenditure unit in the contribution of expanding total aggregate demand. The principal role of city government is to allocate goods and services expenditures and to design a local revenue system, with reference to a municipal environment attractive to industrial investors.

. . . cities attain viability by giving birth to new industries. Large urban areas have the infrastructure and have made the investments in institutions and in human beings necessary to invent, innovate, promote and finance local development to ensure the area's future.[5]

X. LONG-RUN GROWTH DETERMINANTS

The growth of cities in the long run is dependent on the determinants of income Y in the "macro-model." It is assumed that investments by businesses and spending by city governments are "dependent" on, or a proportion of, the level on income Y. Only exports or sales outside the city are independent of income in the local economy. Over the long run, an increase in exports will bring about an increase in local income that will generate increases in consumption, investment, and government outlays. The size of the increase in income will be determined by the relevant multiplier. However, in the long run, dynamic changes occur in other economic relationships in the city. Prices of local and external goods and services, wage levels, and local investment will change. Householders may migrate to other urban areas. Thus the long-term vitality of a city is determined in part by the structure and types of industry or groups of industry, patterns of out- and in-migration of labor and other resources, changes in wage and income distribution patterns, and industrial location advantages of supplies of energy and land.

Over time, shifts, changes, and variations occur in the level of sector spending, output, and thus income in cities.

The traditional emphasis in industrial development in most

---

[5] Wilbur Thompson, "The Process of Metropolitan Development: American Experience," *America's Cities* (Ann Arbor, Michigan: University of Michigan, Bureau of Business Research, 1970), p. 3.

cities has been investment in manufacturing industries and product sales. These industries are capital intensive not labor intensive. The labor-intensive services (wholesale and retail trade, finance, insurance, real estate, general services, and government) historically have not provided as many urban employment opportunities as the manufacturing, transportation, and public utilities sectors. Significant shifts are occurring in the importance of employment opportunities in these two broad types of economic activity.

Between 1947 and 1961, the services sectors accounted for 90% of all new jobs. From 1961 to 1969, the services sectors continued as the primary source of new employment opportunities. Within the services subsectors, general services and government have emerged as the most important growth sectors in urban economies. The percentage gain in urban employment in manufacturing was 20% in the 1960 decade, but general services employment increased 50% and government employment rose 46%. In a representative midwestern industrial city, Cleveland, Ohio, manufacturing employment increased 7% (1960 to 1969), while general services employment gained 46% and government employment rose 42%. The services sector produces no tangible product and is white-collar, labor intensive in employment. The shift in job opportunities from blue-collar to white-collar types has been underway in New York City and in other cities for the last decade. The short-term effects of this shift in employment opportunities should provide somewhat greater cyclical job stability, more opportunities for women, youth, and part-time workers, but the long-term effects are significant for urban economic development.

XI. PROGRESSIVE AND NONPROGRESSIVE INDUSTRIES

All economic activities in urban areas may be divided into two types.[6]

---

[6] Input-output analysis is another way of summarizing and identifying the level and type of economic activity in an urban area and various interrelationships. The input-output technique shows the basic money flows among sectors, but for each industry sector and for households to every other household and every other industry sector in an urban area.

Type One. The "technologically progressive" activities are typified by innovation, capital investment and accumulation, and the development of increasing size (economies of scale). Efficiency improves with increasing per-man-hour of input in these activities.

Type Two. "Nonprogressive technological" activities exhibit irregular increases in efficiency or ouput per man-hour of input.

Progressive industries have relatively rapid increases in productivity. Nonprogressive activities have slow increases in productivity. The fundamental factor in the determination of the appropriate progressive or nonprogressive classification is the "labor intensity." Manufacturing, which employs labor as one of the productive resources, is a type of progressive sector. The output and the quality of the product in manufacturing is a function of the relative efficiency of combinations of labor and capital equipment. Increasing rates of output need not be acccmpanied by increasing labor inputs. Quality is not dependent on the quality of the labor employed.

In selected nonmanufacturing sectors, particularly in the services, the volume of output and the quality of the product is determined by the quality and productivity of the labor input. "Technologically nonprogressive activities are characterized where 'labor is an end in itself . . .' "[7]

It is difficult to neatly classify urban industries into the two different classifications, since many economic activities fall between the two polar cases. "Yet, the distinction between the relatively constant productivity industries and those in which productivity can and does rise is a very real one, and one which . . . is of considerable practical importance."[8]

For example under certain conditions the cost per unit of output in nonprogressive industries may rise without limit. The unit

---

The input-output system is based on an accounting technique that measures these flow of inputs and outputs between various sectors. Input-output relations between different sectors in an urban area are summarized as dollar flows of sales and purchases between and among different sectors.

[7] W. J. Baumol, "Macroeconomics of Unbalanced Growth," *The American Economic Review*, Vol. LVIII, No. 3, June 1967, p. 416.

[8] Ibid., p. 417.

cost of output in the technological progressive industries may remain constant. Thus a disparity will exist between the cost of output between the two types of industry types. Policy measures to modify the inbalance in output may bring about a decrease in the rate of growth of the labor force.

If productivity per man hour rises accumulatively in one section relatively to its rate of growth elsewhere in the economy, while wages rise commensurately in all areas, then relative costs in the nonprogressive sectors must inevitably rise *and these costs will rise accumulatively and without limit.* For while in the progressive sector productivity increases will serve as an offset to rising wages, this offset must be smaller in the nonprogressive sectors.[9]

As a result of unbalanced productivity in the two sectors, over time, larger and larger labor inputs will be used in the technologically nonprogressive sector.

The pattern of growth in urban areas with the two classes of industries depends on the elasticity of demand for products. With future declines in the relative cost of output, and if the income elasticity of demand is high, "manufacturing industries will not increase their share of the labor force and this makes it difficult for an economy to maintain the rate of growth."[10]

In nonprogressive industries such as education and personal services (barbers, beauticians, restaurants, and theatres) cumulatively increases will occur. Such industries will increase the proportion of resources employed in that sector because of more inelastic demand. As costs in these industries increase, total resources used will decline. The services or the goods output will become high-cost, perhaps, luxury goods. Labor- intensive activity, such as fine restaurants and furniture making, may develop a handicraft characteristic because of the disparity or the unbalanced productivity growth.

---

9 Ibid., pp. 419–420.
10 Ibid., p. 21.

Note: For a more complete discussion of macro–markets see F. K. Harmston and R. E. Lund, *Applications of Input-Output Framework Through a Community Economic System,* Columbia, Missouri: Univ. of Missouri Press, 1967.

XII. IMPACT OF UNBALANCED GROWTH

The economic repercussions of this unbalanced growth may mean that (a) labor-intensive service will develop on a handicraft or on an amateur basis; (b) large numbers of products that are very labor intensive may disappear from local markets; (c) costs in activities in the economy will inexorably rise; (d) because of the rising costs, output in some sectors can be increased only by increasing the proportion of the local labor force in nonprogressive activity; (e) the rate of growth in the economy will decline because of the manpower drain from the technologically progressive industries; (f) the real resource cost in the nongrowth industries will increase; (g) only those products that have inelastic demand will be available in the local market.

Even more apocalyptic are the problems of financing urban public services. Many services provided by municipal government are labor intensive. Education, police, fire protection, and welfare services are technologically nonprogressive. Assuming that this analysis is applicable, there is little reason to believe that the recent pattern of financial pressures in the urban public sector will not continue.

Thus the industrial base and drive for industrial development in urban areas in the future will confront the unbalanced growth problem. Unbalanced growth, in the form of incipient problems of resource use and decreases in productivity plus fiscal pressures for public services, may cause the quality of public and private employment in urban areas to decline rather than to improve over the long run.

However, the long-term economic development of any urban area is a function of the dynamic forces that originate with private and public decisions affecting the allocation of outputs and income. The forms of analysis introduced in the previous sections are useful in identifying the factors that determine "macro" conditions in urban economies. These determinants are the basic information needed for the design of public policies to stimulate urban economic development.

4

The Economic Functions of the City

Make no mistake about the genius of the urban achievement. Consider first the sheer technical knowledge and skill required to keep a relatively large number of people alive under urban conditions. The provision of food, shelter, sanitation, and health at levels adequate to keep people alive and productive under urban conditions. . . .[1]

The city is in a constant process of spatial movement and evolution. Class and ethnic groups are constantly engaged in spatial progression through residential areas. The economic base of the city continues in flux and changes location within the city. Areas of cities decline and die, hopefully to be rejuvenated to perform a different urban function. Other areas now grow and prosper, but will enter the phase of decline as their physical facilities age and deteriorate and their functions grow less important or are shifted to other parts of the city.

In addition to spatial motion within the city, there is temporal motion for the city as a whole. Cities go through a life cycle of infancy, maturity, aging, and/or decline. Their functions are altered through time, and their importance within the regional complex of cities changes. The temporal dynamic of the city generates changes in function, structure, and form dictated by social, demographic, economic, and technological change.

Thus the city must be viewed as a dynamic phenomenon. A static interpretation, which is intuitively held by many, even urban specialists, is fraught with pitfalls. It results in remedial solutions that cannot alleviate because they resist ongoing spatial and temporal changes within the city and its functions. It results in rigid urban planning and designs that do not have

ard Reissman, *The Urban Process*, op. cit., p. 2.

the flexibility to adapt to the directions and imperatives of the urban dynamic. What must be considered are the implications of a spatially and temporally dynamic interpretation of the city.

To understand this temporal and spatial dynamic and why cities continue to grow in spite of the alleged urban crisis, it is necessary to examine the city's microeconomics. For the economist the process of understanding the urban environs begins with the question: Why the city? This question can be subdivided into three more specific questions. *First,* what are the economic functions of the city that necessitate this dense agglomeration of men and enterprise? This question explores why the city or urban agglomeration is economically necessary or important as a factor or input in the process of production. *Second,* what are the nature and characteristics of the city that cause it to be a "consumption commodity" desired by urban residents? In addition to a role as an input factor in the productive process, the city is also an environment in which people choose to live, desiring the social, cultural, political, and economic benefits generated within this context. The role of the city as a "consumption factor of production" must be examined to facilitate an understanding of the nature of the urban environment. *Third,* why does a given city exist as a specific geographical location? The answer to the question of urban location lies within the historical origins of the city—the direction and intensity of the development of this continent, geographical barriers, and access ease and positive locations factors, such as proximity to raw materials, market areas, and climatic conditions.

A. The Economic Rationale for Urban Concentration

The urban agglomeration is a significant economic factor of production if it permits more efficient production of goods and services than could be achieved if firms were more widely dispersed. Economic efficiency is measured in terms of physical output relative to cost, or returns from the sale of an output relative to cost. Thus the city becomes an important factor of production if it permits the centralizing businesses and industries to produce and distribute their products at a lower unit cost than would be possible in a nonurban location. Given the empirical fact that firms have tended to agglomerate, what is the nature of the economies achieved by this centralizing process?

B. Agglomeration Economies[2]

The economies obtained by firms centralizing in an urban area may be grouped into three major categories: (1) economies of scale, (2) localization economies, and (3) urbanization economies. Their interaction and sum are characterized as "agglomeration economies" and form the economical rationale for the centralization of industrial and business activities. Notice that many of the economies obtained from increasing urban and industrial size may be exhausted beyond some optimum scale of operation. Urban and industrial growth beyond the optimum scale of functions and operation will result in diseconomies of scale which generate many of the critical urban problems that characterize metropolitan areas.

I. ECONOMIES OF SCALE

Increasing industrial size under given circumstances will result in economies to a firm (see Table 4-1). These economies result in falling unit cost over a given scale of operations. If the demand for the product is sufficiently large relative to these increasingly efficient scales of production, producers will attempt to take advantage of these economies.

Economies of scale are not unique to firms operating in urban areas, but accrue to all industrial operations (regardless of location) if there are economies from an increased scale of operations. To attain any larger scale of plant and operation there must be assimilation at a common point of a variety of productive factors such as labor, capital equipment, primary raw materials, transportation facilities, and the like. For an industrial enterprise to take advantage of economies of scale, attempts are made to locate relative to an urban area that provides accessibility to the desired factor inputs, or to attract these factors

---

[2] Agglomeration Economies have been called "economies of spatial-juxtaposition." Walter Isard, *Methods of Regional Analysis* (New York: John Wiley, 1960), pp. 404–405.

Table 4-1. Economies of Scale

Form of Economy	Example
Division and Specialization of Labor Increasing industrial size permits a finer articulation of production among various stages, for example, the labor force can be divided among the various stages of production and its specialization in specific tasks. Specialization results in lower per unit wage costs due to the increased proficiency of the worker and the minimization of time lost in alternating between functions. "A larger plant with a larger work force can permit each worker to specialize in one job, gaining proficiency and obviating time-consuming interchanges of location and equipment. There naturally will be corresponding reductions in the unit cost of production."[a]	(Meat processing and packing industry preparing beef, pork, and mutton. Major United States centers of this industry are Omaha, Chicago, Sioux City, Kansas City, and South St. Paul.) *Division and Specialization of Labor* Meat goes through 25 operations before it hangs dressed in packinghouse coolers. At the smallest possible scale of operation, one man would have to perform all 25 operations. Increasing the size of the labor force would permit specialization of workers in each stage of production with increasing skill and efficiency. In addition, the time lost in alternating between functions would be eliminated.
Larger Units of Fixed Capital Equipment The ability of a firm to take advantage of potential economies derived from an increase of division and specialization of labor can be limited by the amount of complementary fixed capital (such as plant and equipment) with which the labor factor has to work. In addition, some capital equipment is *"indivisible."* There may be a single optimum capacity of a unit of equipment. Thus the most efficient size is physically fixed. Attempts to use a similar, although smaller, piece of equipment or to utilize the existing piece at less than the optimal rate results in inefficiency or increased costs of output.	*Larger Units of Fixed Capital Equipment* The scale of meat processing plants may be limited by the size of refrigeration facilities, conveyor systems, scalding, dehairing, and grinding equipment, and semi-automatic slicing and weighing systems. Increased utilization of these units of capital equipment would result in greater efficiency and lower per unit costs over a given scale of operations.

Table 4.1. Cont.

Form of Economy	Example
Technological Factors	*Technological Factors*
An increasing scale of operation also permits utilization of technology that cannot be applied in a smaller scale of operations. For example, an assembly-line technique may not be feasible for a very small plant utilizing few complementary factors such as labor.[b] The ability to use more advanced technology with increasing industrial size permits the incorporation of more automated equipment which may reduce the per/unit cost of production. A second technological factor is that the cost of purchasing and installing larger machines is proportionately less than for smaller machines. This installation economy means that expanding size tends to reduce per unit cost of production.[c]	Conveyor system and assembly-line techniques would not be practicable for a very small scale of operations. Increasing scale of operation would permit utilization of this specialized equipment, thus permitting a more complete division of labor, minimizing time lost in transporting product from one stage to another.
Bulk Transactions	*Bulk Transactions*
An added inducement to increased industrial size is lower unit cost of large or bulk purchases of raw materials. Discounts are often available for large quantity purchases, and some resources, such as electricity, can be obtained at special industrial rates.	Larger bulk purchases of meat animals and other factors of production will result in lower per unit costs. "Gas, electricity, and water, for instance, are sold to industrial consumers at graduated rates roughly reflecting the economies of large scale supply of these essentials. Transportation rates on both materials and products go down considerably when larger, for example, car load, train load, or ship load, consignments can be made at one time, and scheduling and other features of transportation service are most likely to be adapted to the interests of large rather than small shippers and receivers."[d]

[a] *Losch,* op. cit. p. 69.

[b] C. E. Ferguson, *Micro Economic Theory* (Homewood, Ill.: Richard D. Irwin, 1966), p. 181.

[c] Ibid, p. 182.

to its location. The latter alternative historically has provided the initial nucleus around which urban areas grew. Increasing urban size provides factor markets and complementary industries that expanding industries use to take advantage of potential economies of larger-scale operations.

II. LOCALIZATION ECONOMIES[3]

Localization economies (Table 4-2) refer to cost savings that accrue to very similar industries or competitive enterprises because of location or centralization at a common geographical point. These economies are unique to firms engaged in similar activities. In contrast, urbanization economies refer to those per unit cost savings accruing to differentiated or noncompetitive firms that agglomerate in urban areas.

III. URBANIZATION ECONOMIES

A variety of economic factors are operative in creating economies for firms engaged in widely differentiated activities within urban areas (Table 4-3). The sum of these benefits is designated as "urbanization economies." The "centralizing pull" of these economies creates clusters of differentiated industries around which urban areas have grown, or influence industries making decisions concerning future location as they attempt to locate relative to an urban area that permits realization of these economies.

Many of the efficiency related factors in urban areas may be termed "external economies." The term is broad enough to subsume many diverse factors defined as "urbanization economies." External economies are benefits that accrue to a firm for which they do not have to pay. These external benefits are available to all firms within the region and cannot be appropriated privately by any single firm or group of firms. The existence of these economies results in savings to all firms and an incentive for busi-

---

[3] These localization economies, although not referred to by that term, are enumerated and discussed in Losch, op. cit., pp. 68–75.

Table 4-2. Localization Economics

Form of Economy	Example
Advantages of Site and Source of Supply Similar or related enterprises may also centralize their activities in response to a local source of commonly used raw materials, or the proximity to the demand for their product in order to minimize transportation costs or provide services. "Or it may simply be attracted by a large market, considerable local demand, contact with government agencies, traffic junctions, or the proximity of other towns."[a]	*Advantages of Site and Source of Supply* Many slaughterhouses are operated either in terminal market cities or close to ranching and farming areas. Those in terminal market cities are oriented to transportation facilities or market areas. Others are oriented to source of supply. Location proximate to resource supply or product demand will achieve economies in transportation and distribution.
Advantages of Numbers and Location Spatial centralization and association of similar industries will provide for external economies such as a large labor market and more efficient auxiliary industries. In addition, wholesale purchasers and sophisticated consumers seek the comparison of slightly differentiated commodities. Centralization permits style, quality, and price differential comparisons.	*Advantages of Numbers and Location* Meat packing plants, clustered at a common geographical point, will attract a large labor pool skilled in this specialized occupation. In addition, supportive industries producing commodities utilized in the process, such as equipment, packaging materials (cans, cardboard, and wrapping), tenderizers, etc., will locate proximate to their source of demand. Clustering also permits retail businesses to compare competing meat products before purchase.
Internal Competition Similar firms may tend to agglomerate to compete for a given local demand market. Thus these similar firms compete for segments of localized demand of an urban area. In this situation, the cost of production and advertising and spatial distance to the next competitor result in a division of a given urban area into market domains of intra-urban dispersed competitive firms. The distance factor creates spatial monopolies or oligopolies.	*Internal Competition* Packing plants located in terminal market cities proximate to the firms to whom they wholesale are in a position to compete for a segment of the localized demand. Location at a distance would necessitate transportation costs to be added to delivered price, decreasing the competitive position of the firm.

[a] *Losch,* op. cit., p. 69.

Table 4-3. Urbanization Economics

Form of Economy	Example
Common Factors of Production and Facilities A major source of external economies is a centralization of sources of supply of factors of production used by many industries and the facilities which play a supportive role in production processes. Perhaps the clearest example of the external economies from clustering of industries is the accumulation of pools of the labor input. In addition, the quality of the labor force in a pool may be improved through time as skills are developed and specialized training is undertaken. The result will be an increasing level of labor productivity and improved attitudes toward work within the labor force. Social welfare gains occur both to the community and to the industries drawing on a labor pool. The presence of a skilled labor pool will create incentives that draw other firms to this location to take advantage of its availability. Reversing the chain of causation, the clustering of job opportunities creates an incentive to the labor factor to locate approximate to the job opportunities created by grouping. Through time the quality of this labor force would be increased. Either process will result in cost reduction to the firms utilizing the labor factor and may represent significant economies to firms.	*Common Factors of Production and Facilities* These factors are similar to the localization economies of site and source of supply. However, this case refers to economies that accrue to improve firms engaged in dissimilar industrial processes. For example, if a meatpacking plant had located relative to railway and refrigeration facilities, an incentive would exist for producers of other frozen foods, such as vegetables and fruit, to locate approximate to these same facilities. The clustering of firms producing differentiated products but utilizing similar production facilities would encourage producers of other refrigeration facilities to locate approximate to these industries. In addition, a pool of skilled labor able to deal with refrigeration and other preservative processes in meats, vegetables, and fruits would develop, from which all firms may draw. This will create economies to all differentiated firms locating at a common geographical point.

53

Table 4-3. Cont.

Form of Economy	Example
Proximity to Supportive and Service Industries Other production inputs provide similar economies; for example, the broader range of industrial and service supportive activities will be created for the primary industrial functions of the regions.	*Proximity to Supportive and Service Functions* Clustering of differentiated firms will permit the centralization of a variety of resource inputs; different firms use similar raw material inputs and similar sources of capital inputs. Most firms could take advantage of existing transportation, communication, and energy facilities. In addition, there would be a range of economies which could be derived from service industries near clustered industrial facilities, that is, specialized areas of finance, business services, advertising, centralized administrative offices, consulting firms, and government agencies.[a]
Social Overhead Capital Social overhead capital provision in an urban setting falls into a category described as external economies. The term "social overhead capital" refers to goods usually provided through the public sector, such as roads, electricity, water, sanitation, sewage, fire and police protection, public health, facilities, education, communication such as television, radio, and telephone. The public services are part of the infrastructure necessary for economic development, since these are facilities for use of industrial firms, their supportive service industries, and the labor forces employed by these firms. The efficient functioning public service is important to the operations of industrial activities and essential to the continuance and functioning of the urban environment. If such services did not exist, private firms would be forced to cooperate to create a similar supply to facilitate functions of all industrial firms.	*Social Overhead Capital* It would not be economically efficient for individual food packaging industries to attempt to produce many of these services. Because of the intrinsic features of these services, benefits cannot be privately appropriated by individual firms, even if privately supplied. The inability to privately appropriate the spill-over benefits creates incentives for single source of supply or public sector supply. In addition to the external economies in these services, there are also significant economies of scale attached which create incentives for them to be provided to the public sector instead of their duplication by a number of firms. Firms and residences find economic bases for services such as electricity, water, sanitation and sewage, fire protection, public services, etc., provided by the public sector. Thus, economies of skill can be appropriated by all parties within an urban area.

[a] Benjamin Chinitz, *City and Suburb: The Economics of M*

Table 4-3. Cont.

Form of Economy	Example
Joint Products	*Joint Products*
Certain industries use resources which generate by-products which are useful in the production of other products. In order to minimize the cost of transferring these by-products to a distant location, industries utilizing these materials could locate approximate to the firm producing them. Other firms might locate nearby to provide equipment for production of commodities from the by-products.[a]	The meat packaging industry creates a large number of animal by-products. Among these are pharmaceuticals and plastics from blood; bone china and gelatin from bones, horns and hooves; air filters, brushes, and upholstery from hair; a variety of leather goods from the hides; anti-freeze, cosmetics, detergents, oils, and the like. Thus firms utilizing these by-products and specialized commodities should be located relatively close to the slaughterhouse to minimize the cost of transferring the by-products and the degree of their decomposition.
Complementary Stages of Production	*Complementary Stages of Production*
A different type of incentive exists for firms involved in successive stages in the manufacture of a final product to centralize operations to minimize cost of transfer or to take advantage of complementarities in the functions, or to integrate vertically into a single industry.	An incentive exists for meat packing plants to attempt to move in to horizontal integration of the stages of production which are located approximate to these stages. For example, many grocery store chains have entered the industry by raising, feeding, fattening, slaughtering, and retailing meat. Economies are obtained by locating stockyards, feeding, slaughtering, and packaging facilities approximate to areas in which the animals are raised.

[a] For a more fully developed example, see Wilbur Thompson, *A Preface to Urban Economics* (Baltimore: Johns Hopkins Press, 1968), pp. 12–15.

Table 4-3. Cont.

Form of Economy	Example

Reduction and Minimization of Costs in Space

Perhaps the greatest incentive for urban centralization of economic activities is the cost of the "friction created by space." Space creates costs of time, transportation, and communications. Thus firms will tend to centralize within the urban core to minimize (a) the costs of time in carrying out the functions of production and transmission of factors and final products, (b) the cost of physical transportation of raw materials and final products, and (c) the cost of communication and coordination. The savings from minimization of these costs are referred to as "transfer economies." Firms will attempt to locate relative to the urban area (a) to appropriate marketing advantages or (b) to locate relative to their natural resource base in order to minimize costs of transferring the resource. Technological developments have tended and will continue to reduce the transfer economies obtained from urban location. More efficient and rapid transportation and communication through space greatly reduce the industrial need to locate relative to resource bases or approximate to urban market areas, but not to regional markets.

nesses to centralize their operations in a given geographical region.

External economies exist in many facets of the urban-industrial interaction. The existence of common factors of production and public or social goods or services in the form of social overhead capital illustrates the concept.

A. *Social Consumption Economies of the City*

The city is a "factor of production" which is an input that coordinates the mutuality of local business entities. It is also a source of employment for the population. The economic impact is more than the sum of the economies and economic opportunities offered to persons and industries. The city is an environment that may be prized for the quality of life, the array of opportunities, and benefits for the creative fulfillment of the individual's leisure time. In economic terminology, the city is also a final product or service which creates consumption benefits to its residents. Men agglomerate to exploit the quality and variety of life that is unique to the city.

Severe as the problems have been, they are compensated for by the achievement that cities—and cities alone—have reached in the development of culture. Science, art, and literature, as well as personal freedom, broad personal horizons, and imagination have been the products of urban environment. Nor were these advances simply the inevitable results of evolution that would have been developed at some time under any conditions. Rather these consequences depended on the encouraging environment of the city, and without it the advances in the human situation likely would have never occurred. "City air makes one free" was the medieval legalism, still true today in the social realm. In the city man found the priceless component that loosened his imagination and gave him the time to apply it to the human situation. The city, in every historical period, has fostered the latest triumphs of man over his environment and of man's understanding of himself. In all ages and areas, from ancient Egypt to modern America, the highest development of human mentality, initiative and achievement has been the urban communities. The history of mankind is the proof.[4]

---

[4] Leonard Reissman, *The Urban Process: Cities in Industrial Societies* (New York: The Free Press, 1964), p. 3.

In the United States, which traditionally prizes rural values, the transition of society into urban concentrations has made the cities the "center of civilization" and the common denominator of our culture. Contemporary political, social, and economic achievements and processes are generated within the urban environment. The cities possess the great centers of education, science, research, medicine, religion, and culture. The cities are the context, if not the subject, of contemporary music and literature. The activities through which men pursue the common life of their society, which are expressions of moral and intellectual virtue, the values that advance the civilization, are now generated within or products of the urban environment.

The benefits for which urban life is desired are many and varied. Some of the claims for the benefits of urban life are the following.

1. *Personal development.* Because the city stands as the focus for political, social, religious, and economic activity, it affords for many a matrix of opportunities for personal development. Given the postulate that man's environment should ideally incorporate the possibilities of maximization of the human potential, the city, perhaps, best provides the opportunity for the realization of the possibilities of human development.[5] Thus a significant consumption aspect of the city is the implicit promise that man can derive a meaningful existence which permits him to confront challenges and opportunities, to explore and understand the possibilities within himself, and to develop his highest potential.

2. *Maximizations of interactions.* Because man's natural proclivities are basically social, he seeks a life framework that allows him extensive contacts with others. The city is desired also because it provides a context in which the interactions of individuals, institutions, and systems are maximized. One thesis argues that "cities exist only because spatial agglomeration permits reduced cost of interaction. Men originally elected to settle in high density settlements precisely because space was so costly

---

[5] At its worst, and for a significant proportion of urban population, the city negates the possibility of development of the human potential.

to overcome. It is still cheaper to interact with persons who are nearby, and men continue to locate in such settlements."[6] By this criterion the city may be an environment which maximizes the potential number of interactions or transactions by which the individual relates to his environment and its inhabitants.[7]

3. *Maximization of opportunity.* Human freedom may be characterized in terms of the alternatives, choices, and opportunities available to the individual. The city supplies the most complex matrix of opportunities in existence. It provides extensive choices in occupations, housing, and public services, such as education and health care. There are extreme varieties and diversities in living patterns and life styles. Leisure time and cultural activities are provided in vast arrays. Available to the consumer is a wide variety of commodities, ranging from the most basic needs to the most esoteric. The urban environment maximizes choices available to the individual and creates the possibility of maximizing the physical and psychological wants of the urban resident.

4. *Public and private services.* The city is also desired because of the high quality level of private and public services. The centralization of men and the intensive division of labor and specialization provides the possibility that the city may provide a level and variety of consumer goods, tertiary activities, such as transportation, communications, trade, government, personal and domestic services, and construction activities that are less expensive than those available in a rural location or supplied by the individuals. Public expenditure also supplies an array of services that benefit the urban resident. The "infrastructure" provides health facilities, education, sanitation, police and fire protection, roads, and a range of leisure and cultural options that are unavailable to nonurban residents. The supply of private and public services is predicated on a sufficient centralization of peoples and activities to permit economies of scale and greater specialization of activities in service industries, and on urban

---

[6] Melvin M. Webber, "The Post City Age," *Daedalus*, Vol. 97, Fall, 1968, p. 1096.

[7] See Richard L. Meier, "The Metropolis as a Transaction-Maximizing System," *Daedalus*, Vol. 97, Fall, 1968, pp. 1292–1312.

governance that capitalizes on external economies generated in the supply of public services.

B. The Economies of City and Industrial Location

Cities exist for specific economic reasons. Economies obtained from urban location and the consumption benefits help to explain the patterning of cities and towns throughout space. A myriad of economic and historical factors explain the location of cities, industries within these cities, and the relationship and interdependence of cities, towns, and industries throughout space.

C. The Location of Economic Activity

Assuming the given pattern of cities throughout space, it is possible to analyze the forces or influences that determine the location of a given economic activity in space. The problem is to determine the profit-maximizing location for an industrial activity among the myriad of possible locations.[8]

The analysis of industrial location concentrates on four central factors: (1) the market area for the product under consideration,[9] (2) the economies of agglomeration to be obtained from urban location, (3) the location of the resource supply used in the production of this product, and (4) the transportation costs, both of the raw materials and the finished product.

The first two factors, proximity to market areas and the economies of agglomeration, create a centralizing pull on industrial location. Assuming that the primary sources of resource supply

---

[8] In approaching location analysis it should be carefully noted that as in all of economics, the goal is not to minimize cost, or to maximize revenues, but to maximize economic profit. Much of the early literature on the economics location was directed toward developing cost minimization models. For example, see Johann Heinrich von Thunen, *Der Isolierte Staat in Beciehung auf Landwirtshaft und Nationalokonomie* (Berlin: Schumacher-Zarchlin, 1875); and C. J. Friedrich, *Alfred Weber's Theory and Location of Industries* (Chicago: University of Chicago Press, 1928); and, to some degree, Hoover, *The Location of Economic Activity,* op. cit.

[9] The assumption of a given market is an oversimplification. Obviously, the interdependence between the existence of some market areas and industrial location is great, that is, industrial location will be a significant determinant in the agglomeration of peoples thus creating centralized market areas.

are not in the urban location, this factor would tend to create a decentralizing pull on industrial location. The final factor, transportation costs, would create both a decentralizing and centralizing pull. The cost of transporting the primary raw materials creates a decentralizing pull. The cost of transporting the finished product creates a centralizing pull. Location analysis considers the benefits and costs, including opportunity costs, of alternative possible locations to achieve a rational and efficient allocation of resources through space.

D. Relevant Market Areas: Derivation of the Total Revenue Curve

The following discussion assumes that (1) consumers for a given product are distributed evenly throughout space and that transportation costs for the product vary only with distance and not with direction (that is, homogeneous transportation facilities through space), (2) transportation costs are borne fully by consumers, and (3) a given individual's demand curve for the product (Figure 4-1) quantity demanded will vary inversely with the price. If the factor price set by the firm is *op*,

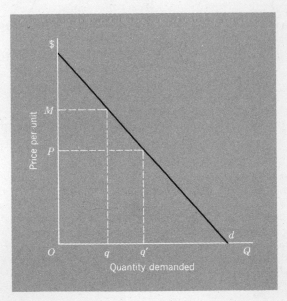

Figure 4–1

the quantity demanded would be q'. The delivered price to the customer, however, will vary with the cost of transportation of the product to his location. Because transportation costs increase with distance, the more distant the consumer is from the factory, the greater will be the price he pays, and the smaller the quantity he will demand. Thus a consumer at the factory will pay op and demand oq', while a more distant consumer who must bear transportation costs will pay om and demand oq.[10]

The effect of transportation costs on the total revenue function of the producer is illustrated by the use of the "demand cone" (Figure 4-2).[11]

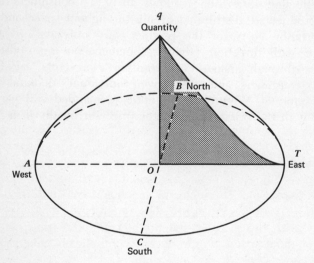

Figure 4-2

---

[10] This result, of course, would depend on the elasticity of the demand for the product. If the demand function was totally inelastic, the factor of distance and transportation costs would not affect the quantity demanded. However, the less the slope of the demand curve for the product, the greater would be the adverse effect on total revenues of increase in transportation costs. The total revenue of the producer would vary inversely with the transportation costs of reaching more distant consumers.
[11] This analysis is developed in Losch, op. cit., p. 106; and Hugh O. Nourse, *Regional Economics* (New York: McGraw-Hill, 1968), pp. 21–22.

The industrial plant is assumed to be located at point O. Points a, b, t, and c represent the four directions and distance from the plant. The axes of the cone are the reverse of the usual individual demand curve. The vertical axis (Oq) is the individual consumer demand, and the horizontal axis (Ot) is the distance in miles from the plant location. At a distance of Ot, the price of the product is the factory price—plus the cost of transporting the commodity over the distance Ot. At that point and price no units of the commodity will be purchased. Rotating the triangle Otq around the axis Oq produces a cone that illustrates (at any given height of the surface) how many units of that commodity will be purchased by consumers at that location. Given a uniform population density and a flat plane with equal transportation facilities in all directions, the quantity of output sold by the industry is the volume of the cone multiplied by the population density throughout space. Total revenue for the firm equals product price times the quantity demanded.[12]

For every factory price established by the industry, a different cone is required. If the price at the plant is greater than Op, fewer units of product are demanded at all locations and the height of the cone as well as the circumference of its base are smaller and the volume less. In other words, with an increased price, the total quantity demanded decreases.[13]

The preceding evaluation is similar to traditional demand analysis, except that the factor of space and transportation cost affects the quantity demanded. The quantity demanded varies inversely with the price of the product and the transportation cost throughout space; the producer hypothetically can derive a total revenue curve for his operation.

E. The Total Cost Function in Space

The preceding section examined the effects of space on the total revenue curve of a firm. The factor of distance will also affect the nature of the total cost curve. The effect of location on total cost is illustrated in Figure 4-3. This model assumes the simplifying assumptions that resource supply for this industry is located

---

[12] Nourse, op. cit., p. 21.
[13] Ibid.

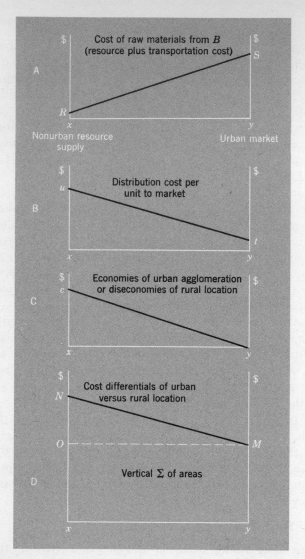

Figure 4–3

at point X, a nonurban location, and the demand for the product tends to be centralized in the urban area point Y.

Panel A depicts the cost of raw materials utilized by this firm, when *a* is the cost of obtaining the resource, and shows the slope of the line as the cost of the transport of the raw material from X to other locations closer to the urban market. Thus if resource costs were the only determinant factor, the industrial firm would locate at point X to minimize the additional costs entailed by transporting raw materials to the production site.

Panel B shows the cost of distributing the final product to the market. It is the cost of distribution at the urban market. The slope of the line shows increases in cost entailed by locating at positions more distant from the urban area. Thus if distribution costs were the only consideration, the firm would tend to locate at Y, the urban market.

The economies of production that would be gained from the location of the firm in the urban area include savings on labor cost, external economies, public and private services, and other institutional factors. As the industrial location moves closer to the urban area, economies are gained until point Y is reached (Panel C). As the industrial location is moved away from the urban area, these economies are lost and accrue in the form of diseconomies or higher costs (as indicated by the slope of the line Ye). If the economies of urban agglomeration were the only factor considered in the location decision, the firm would tend to locate at the urban point.

All three economic factors, however, must be considered in determining a cost minimization location for the industrial firm. Panel D represents a summation of areas under the three other curves and illustrates the cost differentials obtained from urban versus rural locations and intermediate points between the resource supply and the urban area. The cost factors as shown in Figure 4-3 indicate that the cost of the minimization point of location for an industrial firm would be at Y, the urban market. At any intermediate point between X and Y the vertical distance between the lines NM and OM indicate the increased costs that result from nonurban locations.[14]

---

[14] A similar analysis using only transportation costs of final products and raw material is contained in ibid., p. 77.

Clearly transportation costs of raw materials can be high enough to offset economies obtained from minimizing distribution costs of the final product and from maximizing the existing economies of urban agglomeration. If the product is the type where the ratio of the weight of the final product to the weight of the raw materials is low, or where there is high transport cost of raw material relative to the transport cost of the final product, savings from supply-oriented location may offset the economies gained from market emphasis. If, on the other hand, a high weight ratio reinforces the importance of the economies of urban agglomeration in determining a market-oriented location.

F. Determinants of Industrial Location: Profit-Maximizing Location in Space

The preceding analysis has emphasized that the total revenue curve is influenced by the location of the industry in space and shifts upward as the industrial location approaches the highest density point of consumer demand within this market area. As the firm moves nearer to its central market area, the delivered product price will fall and will permit the sale of a greater output through space with an increasing total revenue.[15]

The effect on the total cost curve is less deterministic a priori, and is a function of the centralizing pull of the economies of agglomeration and the transportation costs of the final product as compared to the decentralizing pull of the cost of transporting the raw materials. Thus the position of the total revenue curve and total cost curve will vary throughout space. Hence the location problem is to find that single location in space at which the differential between the total revenue and total cost curves will be the greatest, that is, the position at which profits will be maximized.

Given the data of Figure 4-3, the total cost function will decrease throughout space as the industrial location approaches the urban area. The total revenue function increases as this point is approached. The profit-maximizing position occurs most proximate to the high density market area of the firm (Figure 4-4).

---

[15] This assumes that the price does not fall to the inelastic portion of the demand curve, which corresponds to the dictum that a profit maximizing firm will never price in the inelastic portion of its demand curve.

Panel A depicts a situation at the urban location. Panel B shows a raw-material-oriented rural location. At the rural location, profit maximizing output would be Y. The vertical distance *FG* is the profit made by the firm.[16] This maximizing position may be compared to the profit situation at the market location. Quantity *X* is the profit-maximizing output level. The vertical distance *DE* is the profit obtained by the firm. Profit *DE* at the urban location is larger than profit *FG* at the raw-material-centered location. Thus the profit-maximizing industrial location is proximate to the urban market.

If the cost of transporting the raw material to the point of production is high relative to the economies gained from urban location, the profit-maximizing position could be the raw-material-oriented position. In Panel C the same total revenue curve for the urban location is given, but a higher total cost curve indicates the high cost of transporting the raw material. In this case, the profit-maximizing output level is quantity Z, and the level of profit is the vertical distance *KL*. The profit *KL* at the urban location is less than the profit *FG* at the rural location. The resource-orientated location becomes the profit-maximizing location in space.[17]

With the simplified assumption that the choice of locations lies on a straight line between two points, an array of alternate sites exist between these two points. It is conceivable that depending on the strength of the agglomerative economies versus the decentralizing economies, the profit-maximizing location may exist somewhere between the two points.

G. Determinants of Site Selection

There is a variety of economic determinants of industrial location, but there are also many subjective and institutional considerations. A selected inventory of the factors that may effect site selection is given in Table 4-4.

Thus multiple factors actually determine the industrial loca-

---

[16] The vertical distance between the total cost and total revenue curve is the greatest, and the slope of these two curves is parallel at quantity Y. This indicates that profits are maximized at this quantity of output at this location.

[17] A similar analysis of cost curves is presented by Nourse, op. cit., p. 28.

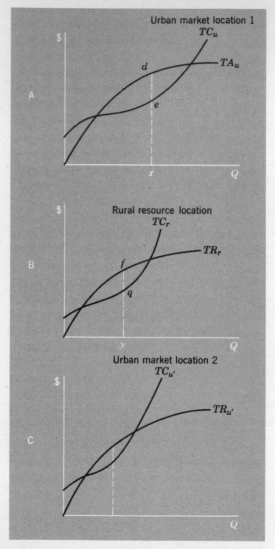

Figure 4–4

tion. However, the predominant consideration of most industrial firms is the maximization of profit.

Hence the pricing mechanism is fundamentally important to the ongoing functioning of the city. Without this mechanism with its disciplinary force, chaos might prevail in the economic

Table 4-4. Factors Influencing Industrial Location

Administration	Labor	Transport Facilities	Educational Recreational and Civic Data	Population Cost of Living and Climate
1. Political party	1. Total Employment	1. Railroads	1. Schools	1. Population statistics
2. Form of government	2. Supply of suitable labor	2. Motor trucking	2. Churches	a. Growth
a. Police	3. Supply of unskilled labor	3. Waterways	3. Fraternal organizations	b. Corporate limits
b. Fire	4. Elements of labor unrest	4. Air Service	4. Libraries	c. Suburban
c. Street and Highways	5. Past history of labor disturbances		5. Parks	d. Labor drawing area
d. Sewers	6. Pervading wage scale for all classes of employment		6. Playgrounds	2. Climate
e. Garbage disposal			7. Theaters	a. General weather conditions
f. Hospital facilities			8. Facilities for recreation	b. Temperature
g. Judiciary			9. Newspapers	c. Precipitation
3. Taxes			10. Special agencies	d. Humidity
a. Rate			11. Hotels	e. Days with sunshine, rain, fog, etc.
b. Assessments, percent of value				

69

Table 4-4. Cont.

Administration	Labor	Transport Facilities	Educational Recreational and Civic Data	Population Cost of Living and Climate

c. Business license fees
d. Exemptions
e. Contemplated expansion of city facilities affecting the tax rate
4. Budget
  a. Income and expenditures
  b. Indebtedness
	7. Minimum, average and maximum hour shifts
	8. Labor turnover
	9. Characteristics of labor
	10. Sex and type
	11. Efficiency of labor
	12. Bonus systems
	13. Seasonal variations
	14. Training facilities
	15. Housing
			12. Hospitals
			13. Public buildings
				3. Cost of Living (per capita)
				  a. Rent
				  b. Food
				  c. Clothing
				  d. Other necessities
				  e. Luxuries
				  f. Department and merchandise store expenditure
				  g. Residential rates on power, gas & water
				  h. Transportation
				    (1) Streetcar fares
				    (2) Bus fares
				    (3) Bridge tolls

Source. These factors are listed in Leonard C. Yassen, *Plant Location* (New York: American Research Council, 1956), pp. 135–146. A more complete list of industrial location factors is available in "Master List of Location Factors" reprinted from the Annual Editions of the *International Site Selection Handbook*, Industrial Development and Manufacturers' Record.

activities of the city. Despite the importance of the automatic features of the pricing mechanism, the density of living patterns within the urban environment creates a significant degree of inter-dependence between residents. Interdependence creates a constraining force on the attainment of socially desirable conditions through reliance on automatic mechanisms.

We can no longer rely upon reaching economically correct results automatically, as an unintended by-product of what individuals do in pursuit of their private interests. We still need all we can get of such automatic adjustments; but there are growing strategic areas in which the power of organized groups is such that, if sound terms of settlements are to be reached, people must consciously intend to reach them. This calls for some understanding of what economically correct adjustments are and a will to promote them rather than pursue self-interests irresponsibly. This element of practical ethics has become an indispensable economic "factor" of production.[18]

---

[18] John Maurice Clark, *Economic Institutions* (New York: Alfred A. Knopf, 1957), p. 71.

5

The Failure of the Market as
a Regulator Decision Maker

I. URBAN MARKET ACTIVITY

The flow of resources into city businesses and the allocation of
products and income to people in metropolitan areas is determined by supply and demand forces operating simultaneously
in many, many product and factor markets. These private
markets may be the source of environment, health, welfare and
other urban problems. The enterprise-capitalistic market system
may produce negative elements in urban areas which are highly
significant in the design of public policies to improve the urban
environment: ". . . many so-called urban problems arise out of
the fact that behavior is not subject to any disciplinary force
such as price."[1] If the market mechanisms cannot allocate resources and income in a manner that improves the quality of
life and environment in cities, agencies of the government must
act as the countervailing power, mediator, or arbitrator to compensate for market failure.

II. RATIONALE FOR GOVERNMENT ACTION

The need for government intervention is a function of the structure and performance of the existing markets and the limits to

---

[1] W. R. Thompson, *A Preface to Urban Economics* (Baltimore: Johns
Hopkins Press), p. 5.

which the market mechanism can deal with the problem of negative effects and social costs. Micromarket failure can be classified under these four general categories:

1. Individuals are excluded from participating in market activity because of their failure to qualify with social, educational, income or other standards established by the institutions that control market behavior and participation.

2. Social costs[2] accrue to individuals in consuming or using products that contribute to or cause personal harm.

3. Diseconomies accrue to the general public because there is no applicable private mechanism for public goods. Goods provided by governmental agencies bring about production diseconomies as well as uncompensated private costs in consumption.[3]

4. Social costs or negative externalities accrue to the population of the whole as by-products of the production process.

A. Case One—Market Exclusion

In case one, market exclusion, the market cannot function effectively because selected potential consumers and workers are unable to participate fully in existing markets. Because of their level of income, education, asset position, training or acculturation, selected individuals are excluded from participating in the institutional arrangements that account for the generation of demand and supply forces. In urban communities, Negroes and other minority groups are outside the type of economic environment that exists for suburban whites. Evidence in the central

---

[2] The term social costs refers to a wide variety of cost elements. . . . the term covers all direct and indirect losses suffered by third persons or the general public as a result of private market activities. These losses may be reflected in damages to human health; . . . in the destruction or deterioration of property values and the premature depletion of natural wealth; . . . in an impairment of less tangible values. K. William Kapp, *The Social Cost of Private Enterprise* (New York: Schocken Books, 1971), p. 13.

[3] Uncompensated private costs that are generated by the action of the public sector, borne by the private resident in the form of inconvenience, or increased money outlays for compensatory services, and replacement of products or goods are "public generated negative economics or negative externalities."

city area of deteriorated housing, inadequate job access, poor clothing, hunger, poor dietary standards, and poor health care, reflects the availability of public services as well as the economic capacity of individuals. The market for quality goods does not operate in urban core areas. Such conditions or factors affecting urban minorities exclude them from engaging in normal economic ventures.

The urban Negro and other minorities have great difficulty in performing as a fully effective economic man in our metropolitan market systems. The Reverend Albert Cleague has characterized this free market exclusion in the following manner.

. . . I think that as far as the black community is concerned, the capitalistic economy does not work for us because we don't have any stake in it. It just happens that when we got to a place where we were able to do something, we were outside and the concentration of wealth in the white capitalistic setup is so complete now that you can't break into that and with all the other racist elements in American society, we are not only outside of it, but we are frozen outside of it.[4]

In our enterprise system, consumption spending by individuals determines their impact on resource and product distribution. The average black does not have as much say as a consumer about what will be produced as does the average white. Since the black on the average has a much lower income, his level of effective demand is much lower. The lower effect demand means that his influence on productive processes is correspondingly weaker.

On the supply side, the possibility for the black, either as an individual or as a member of a community, to undertake his own production is also less than the white community's. The long pattern of educational and employment discrimination has left the black lacking in the essential ingredient for productively developed managerial ability. Even if financial discrimination were to end, the black would still have reduced access to money and the resources necessary for the financing of productive enterprise. Bankers and lenders of capital operate as economic men

---

[4] Reverend Albert Cleague, Personal Interview in Detroit, July, 1968, Central United Church of Christ.

who are resistant to high risk loans, to untried enterprises operated by managers with underdeveloped ability.

Educational discrimination in urban cores has not inculcated high degrees of technical skill in the black community nor reinforced the learning skills and habits. Blacks have been forced into low productivity, low skill jobs. They have little opportunity for advancement, and are typically "last hired, first fired." This type of employment hurts black productivity and cuts off access to new and different skills and to job training. Even more important has been the pattern of job discrimination. For many years many businesses refused to hire blacks except for low-paying, unskilled, no opportunity jobs, regardless of what the skill level or productivity of the black individual might be. Unions, particularly trade and craft unions, maintain rigid color barriers that have kept blacks out of apprentice and training programs.

Discriminatory patterns have widened the productivity and income gap between black and white. Impartial economic processes tend to reinforce the existing and historical patterns of discrimination. Discrimination in education and job selection affects productivity and economic rewards. Low incomes due to low productivity prevent asset accumulation and, hence, property income among blacks is significantly lower in relative terms than among whites. This has tended to widen the income gaps between white and black.

B. *Case Two—Consumption Based Market Failure*

The second case of market failure is characterized by increased real and money costs from the use or consumption of goods and services. If individuals are able to participate in demand and supply forces in private urban markets, private choice operates to allocate resources for their personal use. Although this system of free enterprise capitalism implies that the consumer determines the flow of resources and has a distinct role to play in the pricing of factors, consumer sovereignty is impotent in solving urban problems. The goods consumed in the urban environments in the United States may, in fact, be increasing consumer disutility instead of increasing satisfaction. The connotation of "consumer the king" is inappropriate because the consumer lacks the necessary knowledge, expertise, and economic power to assure that the goods and services that he uses or consumes are of a quality and design to improve his well-being. A recent example of the consumption-based market failure is the automobile manufacturers' failure to provide adequate safety features. They were slow to make the seat belt standard equipment on American-produced cars. The quality features of automobile tires, brakes, bumpers, and/or the vehicle itself are examples of where social costs are incurred by a consumer attempting to satisfy his utility with a product that has been produced without appropriate societal health, welfare, and safety standards. The unwillingness or inability of automobile manufacturers to produce effective combustion and exhaust systems is another case where the press for profits have contributed to noise, air pollution, and related health problems in urban areas.

The uncontrolled use of DDT and other pesticides has brought contamination of the food production environment as well as potentially irreversible damage to ecological balance in our flora and fauna. The use of cyclamates rose sharply until 1969 when the government determined that its excessive use was a health hazard. Cigarette smoking and other uses of tobacco have been finally identified by public authorities as hazardous.

Thus consumers who buy on the basis of given private market conditions may be using products that can damage their health. Since the consumer is without effective control or knowledge, the allocation of resources for the examples above imply that the only outcome for the consumer is death or incipient high health care cost. The private enterprise market system is subject to control only after the death determinant generates the national publicity which stimulates policy makers to invoke retribution.

C. Case Three—Public Market Externalities

Every metropolitan resident in the United States buys goods and services produced in public as well as private markets. Rubbish collections, sewage collection, and water service are examples of goods and services provided by municipal governments rather than by private sector entrepreneurs. There are demand and supply forces that determine the quality, quantity, and distribution of government services in municipal areas. The market connotation is significant simply because the total enjoyment or satisfaction or the total positive utility of urban residents is a function of public and private output. If the public market operates to provide a high quality of services made available to all citizens in municipal areas, it is generally assumed that the public market functions well. However, when the allocation of resources is undertaken in a public market in such a way that private demand cannot be exhibited, or policy makers fail to recognize private demand for public services, or incur uncompensated costs on residents, the public market is contributing to private disutility. A good example of uncompensated costs or "public market negative externalities" as inconvenience and a decrease in utility are intraurban freeways. Intraurban freeways at peak-load periods have been characterized as the longest parking lots in the world. The reference is to congestion.

Congestion in American cities is a function of the type of payment and allocation mechanism for freeway construction. Highways have been constructed to place thousands of cars in the downtown areas at critical periods during the daylight hours. The federal government has chosen to finance the freeway construction for intracity transportation in such a way that the users, both private and commercial, assume minimum out-of-pocket costs for the use of that facility. For practical purposes, the marginal cost of using the freeways for the average suburbanite commuter is zero. The only effective market mechanism operating to reduce the congestion is the congestion itself. The real cost and incipent money cost of time lost in seeking a parking place militates against using the freeway.

Where governments are the supplier of goods, output of that public market will reflect the extent to which the public officials have recognized private needs. Public markets do not necessarily function to provide adequate levels of goods and services to all urban residents. Additional commentary on municipal supply disparities is discussed in Chapter 6, but the following commentary is instructive of the failures of public markets to provide compensatory mechanism for the failure of private markets.

Watts, . . . , is a segment of that endless, formless, urban mess which, like a stranded jellyfish, rots in the California sun. The conspicuous consumption flaunted under the gaudy skyscrapers of Wilshire Boulevard only emphasizes the conspicuous vacuity under the palm trees of this peculiar suburban slum. There is much in both to suggest the American dream turned nightmare: free, bold enterprise reaching the sky along the "miracle mile," and an absurd remnant of the suburban ideal in Watts.[5]

D. Limits of Market Effectiveness

Existing private sector markets function to exchange the contingent variables or factors that bring about a decrease in the quality of life in our cities.

Air pollution is an example of production externalities or production diseconomies. The market is not able to operate to reduce the negative externalities that accrue as a result of the production process.

E. Case Four—Production Externalities

The social costs identified in the fourth case as a by-product of urban industrialization and market failure can be illustrated in selected economic ills or urban economic ills.

A United States Public Health Service report on the magnitude of air pollution in 14 American cities, based on the relative severity of eight pollution factors, listed New York in the number one ranked position, with Miami the fourteenth. The pollution sources have been putting more than 140 million tons of contaminants into the atmosphere per year. Increases in the volume of pollutants has been caused by many factors including more automobiles, more industry, more space heating, more people, and no reduction in the fumes from refuse disposal and so forth. Psychological annoyance and esthetic factors translate into decreased property values, damage to structures and materials, and damage to crops and other plants, with money costs in the millions of dollars.

Air pollution is specific in locations. There is little likelihood that the negative effects of pollution are shifted into other markets. Air pollution analysis shows the clear impact on land and human values adjacent to particular sites. For example, in

---

[5] Wolf Von Eckardt, *A Place to Live* (New York: Delacorte Press, 1967), p. 28.

St. Louis a study indicated that "property values were linearly related to mean annual sulfation rates. When sulfation rates were divided into eight equal locations of rising intensity, values appear to decline $250 per lot, per zone other things remaining constant."[6] "This would appear to be enough to justify even a costly control effort, but it seems that the disbenefits that people attach to air pollution is finite and possibly fairly measurable. It is not suggested that total prohibition of use of air's assimilative capacity is usually the right answer."[7] Spillovers or by-products such as air pollution have economic costs that are borne by large numbers of citizens in an environment where allocation occurs for the productive use of resources.

Ronald Ridker in his *Economic Costs of Air Pollution, Studies in Measurement* estimated the total cost for diseases associated with air pollution, at $1,989.9 million. Cancer of the respiratory system was the single largest disease cost of that pollution. This is not to imply that all of this cost is directly attributable to air pollution. "If we wish to use economic loss calculations in a systematic way for decision-making, we would need to know not only what portion of existing disease cost is due to air pollution, but also how the various categories of cost vary with concentrations of exposure."[8]

Given the deterioration of urban environmental quality because of the by-products of the production process, economic concepts of the market explain the failure of allocation methods to abate the negative costs of production processes. In the metropolitan areas, individuals are both most adversely and most positively affected by the successful functioning of the market system. Residents of metropolitan areas both enjoy, endure, and cause the output and by-products of the functioning of our market system. The extent to which benefits accrue is a function of income, wealth, education, health, and the like, but the extent to which costs accrue is a function of market allocation.

---

[6] Quoted from Allen V. Kneese, "Research Goals and Progress Towards Them," *Environmental Quality in a Growing Economy* (Baltimore: Johns Hopkins Press, 1966), p. 77.

[7] Ibid.

[8] Kneese, op. cit., p. 77.

A brief review of the micromarket mechanism provides the information for understanding the need for government intervention in market activity.

III. THE MICROMARKET MECHANISM

In the micromarket mechanism, demanders and suppliers are satisfied with an equilibrium market price and a given volume of output. The satisfaction refers both to the amount of resources given up by society measured by the cost of the inputs and to the individual demand for products reflecting consumer preferences. Demanders want the products to satisfy individual needs or utility.

On the supply side, the manufacturer, facing competitive conditions in the resource market, finds the price of the inputs set by demand and supply conditions in factor markets. The entrepreneur pays only those costs of inputs used in the production process. The producer has no way of incorporating nonmarket determined external cost or "social" cost in pricing the inputs or output.

Thus the producer, in estimating input cost, is faced with a dilemma when he is forced to account for costs to society accruing because of the production process.

If, for example, the pollutants from a smokestack at an industrial plant dirty houses or clothes, production costs are exclusive of these pollution costs. The manufacturer through his production process is a causal factor in the changing environmental quality of residents living near the industrial facility. Smoke or dust from the chimney of the manufacturer forces housewives to buy more laundry detergent, forces homeowners to paint more frequently, or causes outlays for medical expenses attributed directly to the existence of a production process. The cost incurred by the homeowner or the parent of a sick child is determined individually by reactions to the polluting production process. Unless there is a form of communication between the manufacturing firm and the resident incurring the penalty, there is no revelation of cost in monetary or resource terms of the manufacturing process. The manufacturer must rely on a nonmarket mechanism to get financial estimates of the cost of his polluting activity.

IV. THE GOVERNMENT ROLE

A third-party legal interdiction is necessary to end the pollution problem. Its solution rests on a legally induced compliance for businessmen. The market cannot provide the necessary information or bring about the necessary action in pollution cases.

The market excludes the information, policing, and administrative devices necessary to end the pollution process. A solutions-oriented policy requires government action at some level. The public sector can set up legal parameters that provide for damages or guidelines for standards of smoke abatement equipment, or that require the purchase of appropriate abatement equipment.

V. POLICY OPTIONS AND ECONOMIC REPERCUSSIONS

When the government enters the market environment to eliminate or attempt to control pollution, government is not neutral. The very reason for government activity in a nonneutral role is to assure that social costs to consumers and residents in an economy will decline. There will be resource allocation effects from government action. This reallocation affects efficiency of resource use or efficiency in the production process. If penalties are assessed or payments enforced by government, there will be income distribution changes as well. Individuals who are forced to pay higher taxes to police pollution or if individuals receive reparations or subsidies from the polluting firm, a different income distribution occurs before and after pollution control. Of importance in the policy options that the government implements is not only the end of pollution or reduction in social costs but the resource allocation and income distribution changes caused by the government's action.

A variety of policy options are available to the government to end pollution. The policy options are economically oriented, but represent legal alternatives:[9]

1. Penalties paid by the polluting firm in the form of taxes.

---

[9] See John T. Wenders, "An Economist's Approach to Pollution Control" *Arizona Review*, University of Arizona, Vol. 19, No. 11, Nov. 1970, pp. 1–5.

2. A privately organized bargaining arrangement between the polluting firm and the injured party for setting reparations.

3. The determination by the public authority of an acceptable amount or an acceptable rate of pollution that minimizes social cost.

4. A payment for the cost or the liability incurred to injured parties by the polluting firm.

5. The purchase and installation of various types of equipment that would end pollution activity.

Given these alternatives, the government has a series of choices to reduce these production source externalities. In the evaluation of the appropriate choice, the government policy makers must weigh the potential results in terms of resource allocation in the production process and of income distribution in reparations and taxes or other payments.

A. Policy Choice One: Tax Payments by the Polluter

The tax penalty payment forces optimality in societal uses of resources. The only way the polluter can avoid this tax is to shut down, try unlawfully to evade the tax payment, or to install a facility for abatement or treatment. In terms of income distribution, the government performs the role of allocating tax monies to individuals through policies designed by Congress. The costs of implementing this program are relatively high because of the tax administration necessary to enforce compliance plus the investigation costs.

B. Policy Choice Two: Private Bargaining
To Determine Reparations

In alternative two, the injured parties receive money payments from the injuring firm. The businessmen reduces his income by the amount of the reparation or closes down. As to uses of resources, the post-bargaining arrangements result in reaching an optimality depending on the cost in transferring money. Private costs result in a transfer of costs from the injured to the injuring party. The injuring party costs of operations are reduced.

C. Policy Choice Three: Public-Determined Pollution Rates

In contrast to (1) and (2), if the government acts to reduce the amount of allowable pollution, there is a zero social cost payment. On a private cost basis the injured party has a lower private cost. The level of operations of the polluting firm is optimal only under certain conditions of demand. The only alternative available for the injured party is a complete shutdown. The distributional effects mean a reduced income to the injuring firm or the industry. There are practically no costs of legal administration. The legal requirement for the installation of abatement equipment has some great advantages in that there is no payment of social cost involved. There is, however, an increased cost of equipment that is determined by the equipment manufacturer instead of by the per unit cost of units produced. If social costs are greater than the estimated outlay for equipment for the polluter, there will be an optimal level of output and allocative efficiency because of the use of the abatement device. The distributional effects follow from an expansion of income or diversion of income to the manufacturers of the anti-polluting devices. Income to the industry buying the devices is reduced by the cost of the device. The cost of government administration is relatively small, since only investigation, legal compliance, and inspections are required.

D. Policy Choice Four: Payment of Liability to Injured Parties

The fourth alternative of liability, if combined with the approach used requiring smoke abatement or polluting devices is instructive.

If the polluter is given the choice of paying either the complete reparation liability to the customers, or of purchasing the pollution abatement device, private costs may be absorbed by the industrialist. Private costs would increase by the amount of compensation, or reparation payment, or the price of the treatment facility. The actual outlay would be determined by the lesser cost of paying reparations or installing treatment devices. With the pollution control device option (also true in the reparation liability case), government administration would be relatively limited. Legal systems for inspection established at the local level would be expanded. Little or no structural changes in government is required. Thus the program could be initiated and carried out with relative low cost and with easy administration. If the compensations or reparations were implemented, or if the firm did not purchase an antipollutant device, the existing civil court system could provide the civil or criminal action mechanisms. There would be no new enforcement mechanisms. Payments from reparations suits would be adequate to cover social cost. The firm might be induced under these options to try to solve its own problems. It would be possible to reduce the reparation liability, or to eliminate the cost of the maintenance of the antipollutant device, if it were able to organize production so that pollutants were not spewed into the air or into the water.

E. Policy Choice Five: Installation of Pollution Abatement Equipment

The reparation option or total liability, plus treatment options in (4) and (5), the installation of pollution control equipment by producers, provide the most efficient solution of all options described. This is implicit in the combination of the choice made by the polluter to maximize gains to society while the firm adjusts its operations to internally assessed or computed costs.

Economists would recommend a combination of (4) and (5) as the appropriate compliance devices to solve the social-cost problem of air and water pollution in urban areas.

For the economist, remedial policies such as options (4) and (5) are acceptable, simply because selected benefits that accrue from the activity created the pollution should be preserved. Pollution is a by-product of productivity. It is assumed that the product is demanded by buyers in the economy. Remedial policy is a trade-off between incremental changes in supply and social cost. Policy should not stop the production or supply of necessary or useful goods for public and private consumption.

VI. GOVERNMENT ACTION REQUIRED

Action is required by political or governmental agencies to implement abatement alternatives. The solutions-oriented recommendation is for third party action through courts or through economic compensation activity. The market provides minimal guidelines for implementing the abatement of air or water pollution. The market system can be used as a basis for determining what the liability should be, but the relationship between the injured and the injuring party is purely legal within the court system or other governmental alternative to the court system. The adjudication process includes a legal assignment of responsibility to the polluting firm to buy equipment that will slow the pollution process.

Basically, the policy alternatives deal with reallocation in the factor market as the result of transfers of money between producers and consumers. A desirable output level will be determined whether or not the factory owner reduces output because of the higher costs incurred from the payment of reparations to inhabitants or by buying an antismoke device or if a government subsidy were paid to the manufacturer equal to the transfer payment made to citizens. The important point here is that improvements can occur through a change in costs and output decisions by the entrepreneur.

In the case of smoke polution, the pollution in and of itself assumes there are some nonoptimal conditions that will persist in society. There are costs that accrue to society which prevent the society from maximizing total resources. In air pollution as well as in water pollution, societal benefits could be increased if the polluting firm continued to pollute until the pollution became flagrant or until the marginal gains to the firm are greater for that one producing firm than the corresponding marginal losses absorbed by other users of air further away from the smoke. If, however, marginal losses exceed marginal gains between the two firms, further polluting activity cannot be considered as beneficial because of reduction in total society returns.

VII. PUBLIC POLICY CHOICES—FUTURE REQUIREMENTS

The previous discussion is relevant to problems of metropolitan America because the social-cost phenomenon is a generic explanation of a variety of urban ills. The ills have operated for long periods with inadequate policies. The social-cost concept illustrated is applicable to a variety of processes that contribute to pollution of our air and water, and to congestion in the streets of metropolitan areas.

The solutions recommended by the economist with the variable options are all within the construct of his theoretical framework. It is questionable whether economically optimal conditions can be achieved in real-world situations when the basic conditions of the analysis are violated through the existence of unequal distributions of income, institutional racism, discrimination in access to markets, and a variety of other factors, including the failure of public authorities to rigorously enforce existing legislation.

VIII. MARKET FAILURE AND PUBLIC INTEREST

The market system cannot work to solve problems of urban social cost without action by the government to direct or influence compensatory policies. The market is without the necessary fundamental mechanism to allocate resources to assure that social costs do not accrue to the public.

The government must play the role of announcing the type, amount, and value of the social cost and must elect alternative remedial policy enforcement. Social cost reduction is thus a function of the ability of the government: (a) to design appropriate social-cost cognitive devices; (b) to introduce effective alternative remedial policies; (c) to expedite vigorous enforcement and funding of the policies; and (d) to rank general public interest and not private interests as the top priority in governmental resource allocation.

The record of social cost abatement in our cities is not particularly meritorious. The market interdiction role of the governmentment has not been readily accepted by the business community. Government priorities in "social cost" areas have limited enforcement success because of the slow pace of criteria design and enforcement funding. The federal government's role is basically that of acting in enforcement only if all other recourse at the local level has resulted in physical and ecological damage.

IX. PUBLIC POLICY ENVIRONMENT[10]

It is apparent from the taxonomy of problems facing the urban areas either as slums, housing problems, water pollution, or other factors in the decline environmental quality of cities that the public forces traditionally included in the scope of an effective market function are inoperative.

At this juncture, however, it is important to notice that Congress bears responsibility for the appropriate "government policy" actions in alleviating the social-cost elements.

Current criticism of the scope and magnitude of federal action can be explained, in part, by the "stage of development of the legislative arts" in dealing with urban policy.

In a careful study at the Brookings Institution, the legislative processes involved in setting national policy (for seven areas of urban problems), were evaluated. The Brookings researchers noted that:

. . . there is little evidence that Congress has developed regular patterns of decision making where urban problems are concerned. . . .

Members of Congress typically have not yet developed stable frames of reference through which to approach the analysis of urban problems. Not infrequently, important urban dimensions are shunted aside as a congressional committee pursues some other aspect of the policy proposal before it. Definitional and conceptional confusion surrounds the idea of urban problems as a policy sector. In comparison to established policy fields like agricultural policy, labor policy, or foreign trade policy, urban affairs policy appears vague and hopelessly diffuse.[11]

It is not possible to produce remedial urban solutions or "economically adequate" policies, automatically or autonomously through the market mechanism, or from individual consumer or managerial behavior directed toward private satisfaction or

---

[10] For a more complete discussion of pollution control see R. M. Solow, "The Economist's Approach to Pollution and It's Control," *Science,* Vol. 173, August 6, 1971, pp. 498–503, and T. D. Crocker and A. J. Rogers, *Environmental Economics.* Hinsdale, Illinois: The Dryden Press, 1971, pp. 113–139.
[11] See F. N. Cleaveland and Associates, *Congress and Urban Problems* (Washington: Brookings Institution, 1969), pp. 358 and 375.

self-interest. But the price market mechanism is the only functioning allocative service available in our society. Society needs all and whatever benefits generated from automatic market decisions. Given the strategies of oligopolist and interest groups, consumers and the "general public" need to consciously reorient their market behavior to redress the costs that stem from excessive market power. The consumers and general public must understand what results or benefits can accrue from market determined allocation and pricing decisions, and what future alternative policies will produce more societal benefits. If consumers or the general public continue to pursue their narrow self-interest, the existing urban policies will place urban areas on a disaster course.

Examples of urban problems and the impact of current and past public policies are discussed in the next four chapters which examine urban public finance, housing, transportation, and related topics.

PART TWO

Urban Economic Problems

6

Urban Public Services—Costs and Revenues

City or municipal governments represent one tier in the super-structure of local government entities. There are approximately 20,000 local government units within standard metropolitan statistical areas in the United States. Each has power to expend monies collected from a variety of local tax and fee sources. A distinguishing characteristic of the governmental structure of urban areas is the extremely large number of different political organizations that are responsible for the allocation of public goods and services. For example, in the New York metropolitan area there are more than 1000 different governments within 50 miles of Manhattan. Similar diversifications and disparities in the number of organizations can be cited for almost any metropolitan area in the United States.

In your own case, your college is probably located in an urban area. That urban area contains a center city and a ring of suburban cities. Your home may be in a *city* which is a suburb with a different political boundary than the *school district* where you attended high school. Your home is probably in a *water district,* or *irrigation district* and, perhaps, a *recreation district,* as well as within a *township* and in a *county.* This taxonomy of overlapping governments represents a source of difficulty in the provision of public goods and services—the chief function of municipal governments.

In addition to the multiplicity of organizations, another characteristic of municipal governments is the omnipresent financial squeeze between revenues and rising costs. This financial squeeze, although a function of a variety of factors, sharply limits the capacity of municipal governments to provide the necessary supply of goods and services.

I. EXPANSION AND COSTS

Since 1965 local government expenditures have accelerated from the rapid rate of increase for the previous ten years. Dramatic increases in these outlays have occurred for public welfare and higher education. Spending on health and hospitals also have risen very sharply. These private services publicly provided are essentially similar to most privately financed services in the sense that, as incomes increase, people allocate increasing amounts of their income to consumption of government services.

The problems in the cities have accelerated the pressure for increases in both the scope and quality of public services. It is assumed that some increases in public spending are complementary to expanding populations in suburban areas. As the private sector has been required to produce a higher volume of goods and services because of the larger number of more prosperous individuals and families, the public sector has faced the same pressure. But the increase in the amount of local, particularly municipal, expenditures outlay is attributable to other factors. The other factors are not, however, inefficiency in municipal administration in the budgeting process, the design of expenditures, or in a lack of frugality in expenditure management. More fundamental in the expansion of local government expenditures are factors that relate to size and population density relationships within urban areas.

There is a relatively static technology in the production of local public services. This economic characteristic is advanced as a reason for the cumulative increases in the relative costs of providing the public services that have this characteristic. The slow change in technology is an explanation of the fiscal problems of big city governments. Rising unit costs[1] have probably

---

[1] Bradford, Malt, and Oates, "The Rising Cost of Local Public Services: Some Evidence and Reflections,' *National Tax Journal,* Vol. XXII, No. 2, June 1969, p. 201.

been the single most important source of recent increases in local budgets.

During the period since World War II, current cost per pupil in public elementary and secondary schools, expenditures per patient day in public hospitals, and per capita spending on police and on fire protection have risen at annual compound rates of roughly 5 to 7%, as compared to an annual increase in total local government spending of almost 9%.[2]

Unit-cost increases are in part attributable to improvement in the quality of services. Increases in the quality of service have not occurred in the direction of reducing costs. In other words, the rising prices of inputs plus quality changes have been the dominant characteristic of the pattern of utilization of resources for the provision of central city government.

In a report of the Advisory Commission on Intergovernmental Relations, the relationship between size, population, density, and per capita public expenditures was analyzed. That agency indicated that in communities ranging from 25,000 to 250,000 in population there were relatively few examples in which the population or density were important influences on per capita expenditures and employment. Up to, at least, the 250,000 level, cities do not, in general, demonstrate any tendencies toward major economies or diseconomies of scale.[3] The Advisory Commission reported also that in the larger cities in Ohio, Texas, and New Jersey, for example, there were tendencies for population size to be related to higher per capita public spending and employment. The commission cautioned the reader about drawing general conclusions, since there were so few cities included in the study. What factors explain the cumulative upward spiral in municipal expenditure patterns? It is difficult to generalize on this issue, but expenditure determination studies emphasize the cost considerations and minimize demand considerations. In terms of cost, historical and empirical evidence supports the fact that expenditures and costs are rising.

---

2 Ibid., p. 201.
3 Advisory Commission on Intergovernmental Relations, *A Commission Report: Urban and Rural America: Policies for Future Growth* (Washington, D.C., April 1968), p. 52.

II. MUNICIPAL SIZE AND COSTS

Other studies dealing with economies and diseconomies of scale indicate that the cost-curve characteristics for a variety of public services reflect a variety of characteristics. Research results lead to the serious consideration of uniqueness of the evaluation made in the ACIR report on cities of 25,000 or 250,000 people.

Residents of cities of more than about 75,000 are unlikely to find expenditure patterns occurring in the provision of public services which reflect any results of decreasing cost or economies of sale. However, a few specialized utility activities are carried out by relatively small as well as large cities that will have a decreasing cost characteristic over a range of output or services.

III. ECONOMIES OF SCALE IN PUBLIC SERVICES

Studies indicate a pattern of decreasing and rising costs for specific services within certain size municipalities. Costs do change with different-size operations for publicly and privately provided goods and services. Economies of scale are of significance in the provision of public goods only as a community grows from a small to an intermediate size. Cities or other service areas that have from 100,000 to 150,000 population, may have an advantage in terms of efficiency in the provision of municipal services. Selected public services that have several different sequential production levels, such as water supply and sewage disposal, do reflect substantial economies of scale until the area to be served is very large. Outlays for chemicals and materials, and capital equipment for a large sewage treatment plant are higher than those for small or medium treatment plants, but the output of the larger plants is less costly on a unit basis.

Two analysts studied operating costs of secondary sewage plants in an eastern seaboard state in the late 1950s. The researchers found a substantial decrease in the cost per million gallons of sewage treated as the plant size increased.[4] This scale

---

[4] Walter Isard and R. E. Coughlin, *Municipal Costs and Revenues Resulting From Community Growth* (Chandler-Davis Publishing Co., Wellesley, Mass., 1957), p. 76.

economies study indicated rapid changes in unit cost levels in plant capacity up to 1.5 million gallons per day, and less rapid cost changes as the size of the operation was increased beyond the 1.5 million gallon per day level. In a study of the cost of operating sewage treatment plants in Toronto, cost differentials related to size or volume of operation were also in evidence. In one plant, with a daily capacity of 3 million gallons, the cost was $55 per million gallons. At another plant, with 50 million gallons per day capacity, the cost per million gallons was $33.[5]

Other studies supply evidence that police functions may be more efficiently offered in large rather than in small areas. The metropolitan Toronto consolidation of police chiefs and boards in 1957 produced economies of operation. The new administrative structure, which substituted a single police chief and four deputy chiefs for 13 police departments in the area, reduced administration costs. Policemen were relieved of clerical and administrative duties for functions of protection of persons and property. After the consolidation, the quality of police protection improved and the distribution of police services throughout the entire area was more equitable, since there was an improved capacity to provide specialized services and equipment to all of the metropolitan area.

The available fragmentary evidence on the cost characteristics of other municipal services suggests that economies of scales may be available in the administration of public school systems. However, there may be no economies of scale in school expenditure other than for administration purposes and little, if any, economies of scales in the provision of fire protection or the collection of garbage and rubbish. There may be economies of scale in the provision of conventional water supply and sewage operations within limited ranges of capacity.

Economies of scale may occur if the expansion of public facilities occurs in communities with excess capacities. In a United States Department of Commerce study, Wheaton and Schussheim indicated that for elementary schools, trunk sewers, water lines and fire stations, the unit investment cost declined simply

---

[5] A. H. Stocks, unpublished Ph.D. dissertation at the State University of New York, Buffalo, February 1963, pp. 280 and 281.

because these services served more and more households. In one residential-area example, total outlays for public services declined on a unit basis from $4500 per dwelling in a development of 100 homes to less than $700 per unit in a development of 1000 homes.[6] Thus there may be short-run economies in the provision of public services that are associated with population densities or particular population concentration. But population concentration and distribution in large cities escalates the cost of the provision of all services.

It makes sense to channel commercial, industrial and residential development, where feasible, into areas with excess capacity of public facilities, rather than encourage growth in presently unserviced areas or places with inadequate capacity . . . . New firms or households locating in the area of excess capacity will spread fixed service cost among more users and thus lower the fixed cost per user unitl capacity is utilized . . . . Through appropriate land use planning, coupled with effective zoning provisions, it is possible to avoid much of the cost of "leap frog" development and thus promote efficiency in the public sector.

. . . In addition to these economic considerations, several political-administrative issues should influence decision making in the provision of public goods, especially in determining the government level for appropriate performance or financing . . . . Municipal performance appears desirable for those public functions not subject to important externalities or economies of scale.[7]

IV. WHICH GOVERNMENT—WHICH SERVICE?

Laissez-faire advocates argue that the best government is the government closest to home. This cliche has value in determining which level of government should be responsible for providing which local goods and services. The political implication is in

[6] William L. C. Wheaton and Morton J. Schussheim, *The Cost of Municipal Services in Residential Areas*, United States Department of Commerce, HHFA, Washington, D.C., 1955, p. 92.

[7] Anthony H. Stocks, *Considerations of Scale in Providing Local and Public Goods*, Bureau of the Business Research College of Commerce, West Virginia University, Morgantown, West Virginia, June 1968, p. 29.

terms of ready access to elected officials who are responsive to individual needs. The economic implication is different.

Goods and services provided by the government have spatial limitations. That is, the range of the benefits of the goods and services is limited on the geographical basis. Police and fire protection are local government functions that extend only to the political boundaries. Police protection in New York City is of negligible value for the protection of homes in Chicago's suburbs. Accordingly, if the benefits for police are individualized in the New York area, residents of Chicago should not pay for New York police protection.

The extent or limit of the benefits determines which governmental unit should provide the good or service. But the benefits from selected government goods spill over the political boundaries of given governmental units. Other goods and services provide benefits to people other than those who pay the tax price for the good or service. Services and goods with spillover effects in either "value or worth" of service or geographically are called quasi-public goods.

Education is an example of a quasi-public good or a spillover effect. Part of the value of education can be individualized in terms of better job access and higher potential lifetime earnings. But there are benefits that accrue to the whole community attributable to the presence of an educated constituency. Individuals educated in one city school district may not work or live in that same school district after graduation. In the case of college-level educational services, there is great in-and-out mobility of the students. Where they get their education is not the same political subdivision as where they finally contribute productively to their own personal welfare. Because benefits of educational services are not limited, it makes little economic sense to have education paid for by taxes tied exclusively to one political subdivision. It may be argued that it is more rational to have local control of curriculum schedules to suit local conveniences, but higher level political agencies should be responsible for the provision of educational services. The spillover benefits would suggest that either higher levels of governments should be responsible for the provision of services, or that there should be a flow of intergovernmental aid between governments to insure against interdistrict fiscal differentials in local services. But intergovernmental transfers may be justified only if residents are not able to move freely between political subdivisions.

Equal benefits throughout the range of spatial limitations provide the basis for assigning tasks for various governments in the most efficient way. As spillovers between jurisdictional areas occur, it may be assumed that all benefits are equal between all equally wealthy districts. The offsetting of unequal spillovers should be done by a larger central government. The focus is primarily efficiency at each level of government and the ability of each government to fulfill its economic responsibilities. Thus the concept of benefits and the spatial limitations of the benefits of the service are a useful but general guideline to delimiting the scope of activity at various governmental levels.

V. INTERGOVERNMENTAL COORDINATION

The problem of intergovernmental coordination is the lack of revenue for carrying out municipal functions. The crisis in local government finance and administration may, in fact, be a crisis in state and local government relationships. The state and local governments may have abdicated mutual responsibilities in approaches to urban financial crises. The crisis dimension is significant simply because any changes that might occur in the environment of core areas or in job access, employment opportunities, and/or other means to increase the participation in the mainstream of economic activity for minority groups are dependent on improvements in the quality of services provided by municipal governments.

There is no market mechanism available to reallocate resources between central cities and suburban areas.

VI. URBAN CORE EXPLOITATION THESIS

The "exploitation thesis" which assumes that the central city residents bear a larger share of the total metropolitan cost for public services is a significant factor in the spatial equity issue. Studies made as early as 1940 indicated that the per capita public expenditures of 76 central cities with 100,000 or more population were positively correlated with the percentage of standard metropolitan area population residing outside the central city.[8] The Hawley study indicated that urban core residents were bearing a financial burden of extensive costly service facilities in the central city, which were used regularly by populations more than twice as large as the central city population itself.[9]

In the chronology of studies on the suburban exploitation thesis, research in the 1950 decade indicated that per capita expenditures of governments of 40 cities with more than 250,000 population were "negatively correlated with the ratio of the central city population to the standard metropolitan statistical area population."[10]

In a more recent study, an analyst reviewing costs and benefits of provision of services in the Minneapolis-St. Paul, Minnesota area indicated that "no conclusive evidence can be found to support charges that either the core cities of Minneapolis-St. Paul or their suburbs in Hennepin or Ramsey Counties, respectively, are subsidizing the other to an appreciable extent."[11]

In a recent study of the Detroit metropolitan area, the analysis indicated that six suburban communities in the metropolitan area did enjoy a considerable "welfare" gain through the public sector from Detroit. Welfare in this context refers to positive benefits from the provision of public services compared to the tax-cost services.

For a family of four this welfare gain is estimated to range from nearly seven dollars to over fifty dollars a year. These figures are averages for the suburban community. For some families there may well be no gain; for others, with frequent contact with Detroit, the

---

[8] Amos H. Hawley, "Metropolitan Population and Municipal Government Expenditures in Central Cities," *Journal of Social Issues,* Vol. VII, 1951, p. 107.

[9] Ibid.

[10] C. Harvey E. Brazer, *City Expenditures in the United States,* National Bureau of Economic Research, New York, 1959.

[11] James M. Banovetz, "Governmental Costs, Burdens and Service Benefits in the Twin Cities Metropolitan Areas," Public Administrations Center, University of Minnesota, Minneapolis, 1965, p. 29.

welfare gain is undoubtedly much larger. Thus, the one obvious conclusion that emerges from this analysis is that the tax contribution of suburban residents to the central city can be markedly increased without offsetting the welfare gain they are currently enjoying from the central city public sector.[12]

The existing research data on the central city exploitation thesis have not conclusively proved that the exploitation conditions do exist in metropolitan areas in all parts of the country. The studies, however, indicate that there are fundamental problems of equity in the provision of municipal services between the poor in central cities and the people with higher incomes in suburban areas. Existing evidence of the spatial inequities indicates the need for additional research knowledge and careful application of equity norms through rational economic analysis of differential public services.

VII. FISCAL DISPARITIES

The fiscal disparities within the metropolitan area itself are compounded by fiscal distortion inside and outside of urban areas in the United States. In this country the total local government expenditures on a per capita basis are about 33% higher in a metropolitan area than in nonmetropolitan areas. This is particularly significant if it is recognized that this is a percentage of differentiation much greater than the difference in personal income per capita or taxable property values between metropolitan and nonmetropolitan areas. The principal factor in the higher level of urban spending is the more extensive and intensive requirements for public services that occur in areas with dense population. The requirement for higher expenditure for services occurs in almost all local government metropolitan functions with the exception of street management and education. Highway expenditures seem to be lower in metropolitan areas while education expenditures tend to be about the same in metropolitan and nonmetropolitan areas.

---

[12] William B. Neenan, "Suburban-Central City Exploitation Thesis: One Cities Tale," *National Tax Journal*, Vol. XXIII, No. 2, June 1970, p. 139.

In regard to revenue there has been a steady increase in local tax levels from non-metropolitan areas to central cities with central cities being nearly twice as high on a per capita basis as non-metropolitan areas and 38% higher than those from outside the central city. The tax differences are greater, proportionately, than expenditure differences, and the gap is largely expanded by the pattern of intergovernmental aid. The least aid is received by central cities and the most by non-metropolitan areas. The differential in aid between metropolitan and non-metropolitan areas is consistent with the differences in aid between central cities and their outside areas. In this case it is the outside central cities areas that do better despite the fact that their resources, as measured by income, are greater than those possessed by the central city.[13]

The report of the National Commission on Urban Problems documents the growing disparity in the relative fiscal capacity between central cities and suburbs. The higher expenditure needs in the cities are significant factors in the cities' capacity to deal with local problems. Three fundamental factors were cited as contributing to the fiscal problems in metropolitan areas: (1) the central city is where the poor and disadvantaged tend to be concentrated. These are high-cost citizens from the point of view of requiring poverty-linked services such as public assistance, hospital care, housing, and other social services. (2) Population concentration increases the scope of costly functions such as police and fire protection, sanitation, recreation, and parks. In metropolitan central cities these kinds of services, as well as highway and traffic systems, must meet the needs of a large daytime population plus a net inflow of suburban commuters. (3) The central cities developed before suburbia, and their public facilities and sewage include a higher percentage of deteriorated structures which need replacement or renovation. These factors, plus others, mean that most central city areas have higher costs than the average area in the suburban fringe.

As costs and expenditures increase over the near short term, the ability of municipalities to provide needed services rests with the future pattern of revenue flows.

---

[13] Alan K. Campbell and Seymour Sacks, *Metropolitan America* (New York: The Free Press, 1967), p. 1972.

VIII. MUNICIPAL FINANCES

Municipal governments and other local governments are able
to use revenue from those sources that are not prohibited by
constitutional restrictions, legislative enactments, local ordi-
nances, or city charters. Local governments may have a constitutional or legislative inability to collect sufficient revenue from
existing sources to finance local services. The implication of in-
adequacy of local revenue sources is, in part, justified if the
increased reliance on intergovernmental revenues and the massive increases in local government debt are taken into consideration.

A. Revenue Sources—Taxes and Transfers

The primary source of local tax revenues is property tax, a type
of tax that has been traditionally criticized as the most poorly
conceived tax ever applied. The property tax exhibits lack of
flexibility or rigidities because of constitutional prohibitions
that primarily stem from debt limitations.

B. The Local Tax Base for Municipal Revenues

The heavy dependence on real and personal property taxes by
the municipal taxing jurisdiction apparently tends to restrict
the level of public services to less than desirable levels.

About five-sixths of all local revenues from metropolitan areas
come from the property tax. If state and other local government
transfers and nontax revenues are included, the property tax
accounts for nearly one-half of all metropolitan government
revenue. And at the city level the property tax supplies almost
as much revenue as all other state and local taxes combined.
This heavy dependence on property taxation is interpreted as
an element in the urban fiscal crisis.

The property tax has been blamed for problems that may
not be inherent in this type of revenue means but, instead, arise
out of metropolitan fragmentation. Government maladministra-
tion rather than the tax itself may be the cause of intrametro-
politan fiscal disparities. The property tax is loaded with defects
and militates against the current heavy reliance on the tax or

the additional use of the tax for providing the financial base for metropolitan areas.

C. The Property Tax

The principal problems of the property tax are well identified. The tax creates a disproportionately heavy burden on housing and homeowners. The burden is perverse because housing is considered a necessity and a desirable form of private consumption of private investment. The administration of the tax tends to militate against the adequate maintenance of urban housing. In terms of income distribution effects, it is regressive and places a heavier burden in relation to income on poor families than on families of higher income. Current administration is inadequate, including very serious violations of the doctrine that all taxable property should be assessed uniformly in relation to its value.

D. Focus on Property Taxes

The Commission on Urban Problems indicated the property tax's significance regarding the urban financial crisis by devoting several chapters of its 1968 report to this tax and its administration. The commission reported that the "heavy load which property taxation so widely places upon housing is a result of (1) the large sums needed for central public services in urban areas, where this type of tax is generally the predominant financing source, and (2) the fact that residential property makes up about half of the total tax base in these areas." As a result,

. . . property taxes average about 19% of the rental value of non-farming housing in the United States currently, equivalent to an excise tax of nearly 24% on rental value, excluding property taxes . . .

. . . [Property] taxes as a percentage of actual cash outlay of housing ranged—excluding the south—from sales tax equivalent rates of 18% for large apartment houses outside of New York City to 30% or more for single family housing in the northeast, and multi-family property in New York City . . . . These very high tax rates are greatly in excess of the rates applicable to other forms of consumer expenditures, with the exception of the taxes on liquor, tobacco and gasoline . . . . *It is simply inconceivable that, if we were starting to develop a tax system from scratch, it would single out housing for extraordinary high levels of consumption taxation.* More likely, we would exempt housing entirely from taxation, just as many states exempt food from the sales tax.[14]

Present property taxes on both land and improvement are not neutral but tend to discourage investment in buildings. A switch to exclusive site valuations would tend to have strong land use defects.[15]

Netzer's evaluation of remedial action in the case of the property tax suggests that policy makers should:

. . . call for the virtual elimination of local property tax support for all poverty-linked public services, including public assistance costs, . . . other public welfare costs, health and hospital services for the poor, and the extra cost of local educational programs aimed essentially at the poor and disadvantaged. At present local tax supported expenditures for poverty-linked services are equal to at least 10% of the total property tax revenues on a nationwide basis and substantially more for the large city. Increased federal and state aid sufficient to eliminate this would make the property tax a more rational instrument of national public policy (by reducing its contradictory income-distribution role) and, at the same time, would reduce the adverse impact of the property tax on new investment in central cities.[16]

Any deescalation of the use of property taxes should have the tendency to reduce the land use and location effects of locally applied taxes. Such a reduction in dependence on property tax could also be achieved through a reform of the property tax. Despite the criticisms of the local property tax, the need seems to be for a type of local tax that has a broader geographical base.

IX. NONTAX REVENUES

There are, however, public services provided by municipal governments that are not dependent on subventions or other taxes

----

14 *Report for the National Commission on Urban Problems,* Part IV, "Government Structure, Finance and Taxation," Chapter 3, p. 11.
15 Dick Netzer, "The Property Tax Case for Federal Revenue Sharing," in *State and Local Problems,* pp. 96–97.
16 Ibid., p. 98.

from other levels of government. Examples of these autonomous municipal services are fire protection, recreational facilities, public utilities, and sanitation. The revenue for some of these local government services are designed on the basis of cost of service finance. The amount of revenue derived from charges for these services and the quality of these services are closely related. The provision of these local services as a revenue source has masked the need for local officials to differentiate between service charges as revenue sources to provide services and a basic costing policy to foster rational development of efficient municipal facilities.

Any attempt to assess the appropriate policy in the structure of service rates involves economic analysis of distribution as well as efficiency effects in the level and collection of service charges and in the expenditures for services facilities. An alternative costing process occurs in policy making in the form of tradeoffs between and among equity and efficiency considerations. The equity and efficiency considerations are a specific function of the twofold distribution and allocation process that automatically occurs with the transfer of private decision making over the use of funds to public agencies. In the design and the policy for rate structure, several questions are significant in income and service disparities that exist between suburban and innercity residents.

User charges and other prices operate to exclude certain buyers and to ration the supply of services within the service area. The rationing process is a necessary condition to any market construct. Prices automatically discriminate between nonhomogeneous buyers. Of primary concern is the type, prevalence, and the origins of price discrimination for public services in the manner in which services are rationed among municipal residents.

The benefits basis of allocating cost burdens assumes a *quid pro quo* relationship between the worth of service supplied and the services consumed. Consumer preferences are reflected in the price offer. Cost of supply is reflected in the goods offer. Within the context of the municipal markets, the benefits principle does not rationalize the allocation processes.

X. OTHER TAX REVENUE SOURCES

Another type of tax used by local governments is the income tax. The federal government's use of this tax plus difficulties in local administration have limited the extension of its source. Sales and gross receipts tax has been used increasingly by local governments where permitted. Revenues from licenses, fines, fees, and forfeitures are widely used for local government purposes. In each tax type a subventions process operates. Sales and gross receipts taxes are usually state taxes locally collected and state redistributed. State administration of locally imposed taxes is widespread. Any subvention process requires unique intergovernmental cooperation to identify which level of government should be responsible for the provision of which services.

XI. DEPENDENCE ON INTERGOVERNMENT TRANSFERS

Municipal governments are not autonomous financial entities. Municipal and other local governments are political creatures of state governments. Municipal political entities are given only the residual assignment of responsibilities for governing or governance. The states have practiced a preemption doctrine, which means that revenue sources that have not been elected for the support of the state government may be used by municipal governments if these local governments are not specifically prohibited from using that revenue source.

The financial aspect of limited autonomy is significant in regard to the funds available in municipal areas. City governments relying on their own tax sources are unable to raise the necessary revenue to carry out all public services. There has been no unanimity in debate as to whether or not municipalities ought to be financially independent of higher levels of government. Municipal governments must now depend on subventions from other higher level governments. In the operation of educational services, for example, the city school system may be supported by property taxes which are local taxes, locally collected and distributed, plus a form of aid from the state in some type of state foundation program. Highway and street repair and construction, carried out at the municipal level, may be paid for by a local operating levy from property taxes, but they are more likely to be paid for through the distribution of funds from state gasoline or petroleum taxes. Such funds are distributed on a formulalike basis.

XII. STATE TRANSFERS TO MUNICIPALITIES

State grants in aid are given to local governments with the same kinds of directives generally associated with conditional grants. Revenue that is shared between state and local governments does not reach the local government levels without strings attached. Funds ordinarily are received for a specific purpose. The conditional aids from the state tend to perpetuate particular units of local government and to divorce the collection process from the outlay process. This may result in the submerging of political responsibility. As the situation now exists, any decrease or absence of state aid would almost certainly force the local units of government to drastic positions such as the dropping of service standards, the use of pragmatic designed tax schemes, or the wholesale shifts of functions of the local government to the state level.

In terms of sources of revenue, the state grants are not neutral in regard to the pattern of the provision of local government services. Thus an initially fruitful pattern of a solutions-oriented approach might be a careful evaluation of the existing patterns of state subventions and the rationale for the controls that limit fiscal flexibility for municipal governments.

Constitutional and legislative regulations plus the common law preemption doctrine play a role in the structure of taxes for municipal governments. Legal restrictions limit improved efficiency and increase the flow of funds, or prevent local consumers of municipally supplied services from assessing the actual cost of the services.

XIII. STATUS OF INTERGOVERNMENTAL AID

Because of the lack of action by state governments in meeting local government fiscal pressures, the federal government is the logical political administration to make a significant contribution to increasing the fiscal capacity of municipal governments.

Intergovernmental revenue from state and local sources continues as a fundamentally important component in municipal or urban finance. In the mid-1960s intergovernmental revenue provided only about one-fourth of all the revenue to local governments. Only a small part of these revenues came directly from the federal government. A large part of state and local government payment was financed by federal government grants. State and federal payments to local governments have been increasing very rapidly. The absolute increases are not as significant as they first appear. There have been rapidly rising costs of state and local government services as well as significant increases in the state and local revenues from their own sources. The revenue falling to state and local governments provided by federal grant-in-aids changed only from 13½% to 16½% in the five-year period before 1967. The proportion of local government income from other governmental sources rose only 4.5% during that period. These developments indicate that intergovernmental receipts have accounted for less than one-fourth of the total increase in the state and local government general funds and for only 44% of the increase in general revenue funds to local governments. The rest of the increase was met from taxes or from other local government sources.[17]

The distribution of responsibility as measured by assignment and aid possesses great stability in the overall governmental system. Thus far federal aid, although it has increased substantially, has not basically altered the relative roles of various parts of the system. Nor have increased state governments fiscal totals increased their roles in the total system. The lack of change in relative roles simply demonstrates that all parts of the system are growing rapidly; there is every indication that all will continue to grow. The only distinct possibility for an alteration in the relative roles is for the federal aid proportion to increase, but such an increase will require massive upward adjustment in such aid.[18]

---

[17] *Report for the National Commission on Urban Problems*, Part IV, "Government Structure Finance and Taxation," Chap. 5, pp. 2-3.
[18] Alan K. Campbell and Seymour Sacks, *Metropolitan America* (New York: Free Press, 1967), p. 187.

XIV. FEDERAL AID TO MUNICIPALITIES

Increased federal aid has been and is being channeled into metropolitan centers. Federal grant-in-aid or aid in 1964 was about $5.6 billion or about 55% of the total federal grants spent. In 1970 approximately $77 billion was to be used or allocated in the form of grants-in-aid to metropolitan areas. The principal increases in federal grants-in-aid in urban areas have occurred in what is called community development and housing with lesser increases for education and a variety of welfare programs for disadvantaged citizens. The emphasis of these forms of federal aid is on programs that provide financial assistance that helps localities meet public service needs. A generalized summary of the federal aid programs for urban areas is given in Table 6-1. Although the figure for 1972 was $26.8 billion, the Department of Housing and Urban Development estimated that the total federal financial commitment for urban development was about $38 billion. These HEW or HUD estimates reflect the magnitude of involvement in communities of 2500 or more, including obligations or actual expenditure commitments that include insured loans or insured loans and guarantees. The HEW or the HUD estimates and the tabular estimates do not coincide or are not comparable, and there is a basic fundamental question about the direct application or applicability of the federal aid outlays to the improvement and the quality of life in urban areas.

Any historical review of increases in federal aid to urban areas shows that this aid is impressive. For example, a fourfold increase has occurred since 1961. Of more significance is the amount of money that must be provided to improve the quality of the urban environments.

The Federal government's commitment for such proposals as pollution is not adequate for needed levels of control activity. The record on federal aid to localities is one that bears very close scrutiny. Recent evidence gives no cause for optimism about the commitment of the federal government to deal effectively with urban problems.

A. Increased Federal Revenue Sharing

The National Commission on Urban Problems recommended increased federal revenue sharing for state and local govern-

Table 6-1. Projected Local Government Expenditures and Revenues, fiscal 1966 to 1975 (in billions of dollars)[a]

Year	Expenditures (in Dollars)	Revenues (in Dollars)
1965	55.1	53.0
1966	59.7	57.4
1967	64.7	62.1
1968	70.1	67.2
1969	76.0	72.7
1970	82.4	78.7
1971	89.3	85.2
1972	96.8	92.2
1973	104.9	99.8
1974	113.7	108.0
1975	123.3	116.9
1966–1975	$880.9	$840.2

Source. 1968 Proceedings of the Sixty-First Annual Conference on Taxation, National Tax Association, Columbus, Ohio 1969, p. 434.
[a] Insurance trust revenues and benefits and payments excluded.

ments. Federal government revenue sharing in the past has been in the form of the categorical grant. A grant of this kind is a payment to finance a particular program or type of project tied to conditions and actions by the local government.

Measures have been introduced in the United States Congress over the past few years which suggest an entirely different approach to the distribution of funds. This change would broaden the orientation of the existing grant programs. The basic idea for increased federal financial assistance was given impetus when Walter Heller was chairman of the Council of Economic Advisers in 1964. The idea is that federal government should share some of its growing income or revenue from income tax collections with the states. Heller argued for the tax on the basis of rapidly expanding urban and local government needs,[19] as well as of the improvement in the fairness of the overall tax system. Fifty-seven congressmen in the 89th Congress sponsored or cosponsored 51 different tax-sharing bills. In the 90th Con-

---

[19] See Harvey S. Perloff and Richard B. Nathan, eds., *Revenue Sharing and the City, Resources for the Future* (Baltimore: Johns Hopkins Press, 1968).

gress, almost twice as many bills were introduced. At least 110 members sponsored or cosponsored 90 bills with 35 variations on the tax sharing idea.[20] The early form of this plan suggested revenue sharing only to state governments. The Heller-Pechman plan suggested that problems of public services and financing are most critical at the local level, but are particularly critical in the urban areas. Pechman and Heller, as well as the National Commission on Urban Problems, and the Nixon Administration recommended "a pass-through" allocation that would recognize the legitimate claims of local governments' traditional funds. Under this proposal about $500 million would have been available in the fiscal year beginning July 1, 1970 for local government support. The amount would increase to $5 billion by 1975. The 1969 Nixon proposal for revenue sharing was never reported out of the House Ways and Means Committee.

The administrative interest in this form of aid to local governments was continued in a new format in the President's State of the Union Message in January 1971. In the 1971 proposal, the Administration recommended that $16 billion in federal revenues be distributed to states and localities. Eleven billion dollars was in a special revenue-sharing program. In this special category, state and local governments would receive monies to be allocated in specific categories for specific purposes of urban development, road development, education, transportation, manpower development, and law enforcement. These were not new programs, nor increases in program. The allocation represented a substitution of different administrative responsibility, plus an attempt to reduce or eliminate selected existing programs in each category. The additional $5 billion was to be in the form of unrestricted grants, for state and local general government functions.

In contrast with the special grants, the nonspecific aid would give states and city governments greater flexibility in fiscal planning, plus local control of expenditures and design of distinctive local needs. Increased experimentation in attacking local prob-

---

[20] See *ACIR Fiscal Balance in the American System,* Vol. 1, Advisory Commission on Intergovernmental Relations, Washington, D.C., October 1967, p. 67.

lems which may or may not increase the likelihood of successful solutions is encouraged by the general revenue-sharing plan.

B. Problems in Design

Revenue sharing is basically untested and is not without potential disadvantages. The amount or the proportion of funds that should be reserved for cities is a source of continual friction between city and state officials. It may be argued that a substantial "set aside" should go only to low-income states, or that low-income states could penalize urban states which bear the brunt of the current poverty problem. There is an incipient danger that state and city officials may view the program as a bottomless "kitty" and a unique opportunity to spend money without bearing the burden of the taxes that raise funds. Potential success is limited by the magnitude of total compensation paid to all state and local governments. Most recommended programs are too limited in dollar amount and administrative scope to have a significant impact on the conditions of fiscal deterioration in the urban areas.

C. Needed Federal Action

Dick Netzer, an authority on municipal government fiscal problems, has recommended a series of actions at the federal level that would help to establish a more desirable system of co-ordinated fiscal relationships with positive benefits occurring to metropolitan areas. The Netzer recommendations include (a) the federal government responsibility for all "income"-supported programs; (b) additional financing from the federal government through conditional grants-in-aid and other poverty-linked programs to redistribute money income for purposes such as health and hospital services, social services to children and families, and special education services for disadvantaged children; (c) additional other federal grants to be used only where there exist real and substantial interstate and interregional spillovers; (d) a federal program of "general purpose" grants to states; and finally, (e) a form of federal credit for state and local income-tax payments.[21]

[21] See Dick Netzer, "Federal, State and Local Finance in a Metropolitan

D. Other Federal Action

Any successful federal program must place more funds at the disposal of local governments and in amounts that will provide needed services. The need for increased fiscal resources is paramount at the municipal and county, not the state government, level.

The need for federal programs is symptomatic of fundamental inadequacies in intergovernmental fiscal relationships. Until a basic and extensive restructuring of state-local government revenue sharing occurs, any federal program of sharing must be considered a short-term, stopgap measure. The restructuring of state-local revenue sharing must focus on the local dependence on inadequate, poorly administered, inequitable tax sources. The most important role for the federal government in solutions-oriented municipal financing policy is to force state governments to restructure their subvention processes. The federal government may also find a potent and effective policy for alleviating the financial ills of cities by requiring national uniformity in the administration of property taxes, and in forcing all states to rely more heavily on income taxes.

. . . Confronted with the growing state and local demand for more Federal dollars with fewer Federal strings attached the National Government is bound to develop a quickened interest in economical ways of helping state and local governments to help themselves. Maybe our system of shared powers would be in better shape right now if, over the last twenty years, Congress had taken a somewhat greater interest in helping State and local governments raise revenue and had demonstrated somewhat less interest in helping them spend it.[22]

Context," *Issues in Urban Economics* (Baltimore: Johns Hopkins Press, 1968), p. 471.

[22] John Shannon, "Federal Assistance in Modernizing State Sales and Local Property Taxes," before the National Tax Association, Washington, D.C., July 23, 1971, p. 14 (mimeographed).

XV. THE FUTURE OF MUNICIPAL FISCAL ENVIRONMENTS

There is fundamental agreement by fiscal theorists on the future of metropolitan finance. Expenditures will outdistance revenues (see Table 6-1). By 1975 it is estimated that if local tax and charges increase at the same pace as in 1956 to 1965, local governments, including municipalities can be expected to collect an additional $77 billion. Given this revenue increase, based on that earlier historical pattern, there will be a gap between expenditures and revenues. Expenditures have continued to outdistance revenues and will continue to do so in the next decade. One estimate indicates that at least $975 billion will be needed in revenue requirements for cities to carry out their responsibilities of paying higher salaries to city employees, policemen, firemen, and teachers, as well as to provide for the capital requirements that will become necessary. These estimates are based on no change in the federal aid program, and on the growth of city tax and other revenue sources at about 6.3% per year. The growth of intergovernmental aid estimates are about 7% per year. Capital expenditures will increase about 5.6% per year with total expenditures increasing through 1975 by $262 billion in excess of present revenues and those expected to degenerate through normal economic growth.[23] How will the municipalities deal with the rising costs of government? Weintraub recommends the following alternatives with the precondition that the political administrator will be wary of attempting to get increased revenues from the property taxes. Any increase in property taxes for the slum renewal or improvements for slum dwellers will bring about increased out-migration of middle and upper income families as well as business enterprises, and will probably bring in-migration of lower income families with lower skill levels and incipient problems.

Because of the size of the revenue gap differs from city to city, raising local tax rate inevitably makes the cities with greatest problems the ones with the highest taxes. The average age of buildings in these

---

[23] Robert Weintraub, "Meeting the Revenue Needs of Local Governments," 1968, Proceedings of the 61st Annual Conference on Taxation, *National Tax Journal*, 1969, pp. 435–38.

cities increases as new commercial and residential construction is drawn irresistably to the relatively low-tax cities. Accompanying this gradual aging of buildings in the higher tax cities is a gradual deterioration of working and living conditions, creating all manner of community problems ranging from increased sanitation problems to increased fire potential and a steady depreciation of tax bases. Thus high tax cities are becoming powerless to finance their own expenditure requirements and simultaneously they are confronted by growing socio-economic problems requiring public action.[24]

The categorical indictment of the administration and operation of property taxes plus the economic allocation impact of property taxes militate against expansion or increased dependence on this kind of tax. Alternatives in terms of local government revenue must focus on other taxes on income and increase in service charges.

Any increase in the use fees or licenses may bring about factors that expedite the movement of the entrepreneurial and middle income groups into areas where the fees do not apply. Of more particular interest, it is estimated that increasing the nontax income cannot bring sufficient increase in total income to have an impact on the expected rise in expenditure. The service charge and nonfee sources of revenue or tax-free sources of revenue probably generate an additional $25 billion in new revenues.

On the basis of historical experience it is probably inept to assume that state grants and aids will be increasing at a rate significantly large enough to offset the gap expected in revenues at the municipal levels.

The viable alternative to this problem of the enlarging gap between revenue and expenditures from metropolitan areas is a function of a variety of political as well as purely fiscal adjustments. The most viable form of political adjustment would be to make state and local revenue systems more productive and more equitable through the expansion and more effective use of the personal income tax, the broadening of the sales tax base, the change of assessment ratios, and the administration of the property tax. Of particular importance is that there must be a way of

---

[24] Ibid., p. 438.

reducing the regressivity of the burden of local taxes through tax relief for low income families and a series of offsets against income tax for payment of state and local taxes.

When the nation was less urbanized and less conscious of personal differences with respect to income, education, race and the mode of living, the tried and true tax forms—property, sales, excises—were, at least, tolerable. Today's interdependence —between the rich and poor, cities and suburbs, and the private and the public sectors—demand that taxation be more interdependent.[25]

XVI. BROADENING THE TAX BASE

If the use of the income tax is coupled with an improved coordination between sales and property tax administration, equity features of the local taxes can be sharply increased. The use of per capita income tax credits and rebates for sales taxation as well as rebates for extraordinary property tax payments can make the property tax more equitable and will permit the income tax to be the form of revenue source that induces the equity.

The objective would be to provide more satisfactory financing for both the services that are redistributive in income and those that are affected by externalities. Any standards for area-wide taxation in metropolitan areas should take into consideration the evaluation of more use of income and consumption rather than property taxes. Both the Advisory Committee on Intergovernmental Relations and the President's Commission on Urban Problems recommend broadening of the base of financial support for metropolitan areas. In the case of the Advisory Committee on Intergovernmental Relations, their recommendations include broadening the base of state taxation by more use of a personal income tax and general sales tax which would include an authorization for municipal and other local governments to set up supplementary late rates on a "piggyback" basis. A review

---

[25] See Will S. Myers, Jr., "Measures for Making the State and Local Revenue System More Productive and More Equitable," Proceedings of the 61st Annual Conference, *National Tax Journal*, 1968, op. cit., pp. 450–451.

by states of their pattern of state and local relationships would be essential to provide a more equitable means of state aid to local school financing and the assumption by state officials of financial responsibility for nonfederal public welfare cost and the provisions of incentives to state grant programs to include local structures. In addition, the ACIR recommends a reexamination of state and local governments with the potentiality of user charges to finance public services. The state legislatures could act to improve the regionalization of property taxes for public schools and could utilize larger government levels such as county-wide or several-county taxing areas with the proceeds allocated to schools.

In addition, the state legislatures must take action to improve property tax assessment and to eliminate unenforceable features, particularly in the case of intangible personal and personal property taxes must move to more full value assessment and to publicize and make full information available about assessment ratios and improving taxpayer appeal machinery. The Commission on Urban Problems reported the need for local government tax administration changes, particularly in the area of the property tax. This tax as now administered is a burden on home ownership particularly for low-income individuals. In addition to the emphasis on property tax, the excise tax component of state and local government finance, normally, is regressive in terms of income and places a heavier burden on low-income taxpayers.

There are substantial reallocations and rearrangements necessary in the tax element of financing and providing for local services. It is implicit that not only is there inadequate administration but distributional and resource allocation defects are inherent in the administration and form of municipal tax structures.

If the total financial dimensions of the urban crisis are to be responsibility changes in local government funding to accommanaged, there must be concurrent revenue and structural plish any improvement in the urban fiscal condition.

7

Urban Transportation—a Mobility Problem

Urban transportation systems are designed to provide mobility for people and resources. Interurban resource mobility is generally characterized by alternative, high-speed options or modes. In urban areas, however, local transportation is characterized by declining local mass transit systems, congested traffic on expressway systems, ineffective coordination between transport policies, problems of pedestrian safety and mobility, and a decline in the quality of commuter service.

I. URBAN TRANSPORTATION PROBLEMS

Mobility, transportation, and traffic problems in urban areas have become more acute because of the increasing affluence of urban residents. The current distribution of income seems to have amplified transportation and traffic problems. Increased automobile ownership is a fundamental factor in the decline of public transportation. The increased number of automobiles per family is a factor in the decline in the patronage of public transportation.

Wealthy suburban residents in urban areas rely on automobiles for the journey to work and/or other trips in the urban areas. As a result of the substitution of automobiles for mass transportation, there are fewer users that demand mass transportation. Decline in users because of the increase in automobile commuting limits the ability of mass transportation systems, particularly buses, to provide good quality service. Increased automobile ownership and use has meant that all public transportation systems are in a less advantageous competitive position as to quality of service provided. Public mass transportation is caught in the financial squeeze between rising fares and declining revenue.

During the last decade, inexorable patterns and conditions seem to have been formalized in urban transportation. In the case of commuter transportation, expressway construction has improved the physical plant and equipment facilities for the movement of automobile traffic, but the volume of traffic at peak periods has expanded to surpass the capacity of the enlarged expressway systems. As cities have increased in size and population with decentralized industry, or as average commuting distance from suburb to central city has increased, the effective demand for mass transportation facilities has declined, the cost of offering mass transportation services has increased, and revenue for mass transportation companies has declined.

Patronage on intracity and suburban buses has declined from a peak of 8.3 billion passengers in 1945 to 4.1 billion in 1971. Intracity bus transportation is a symbolic illustration of dilemmas that face the operators of transportation systems and potential passengers. The mass transportation problems of declining patronage, rising fares, rising costs and declining revenues is not a condition isolated or unique to large urban areas. Cities such as Baltimore, Trenton, Portland, Rochester, and Minneapolis-St. Paul have all found it necessary to provide public funds for a declining private motor bus system. Even in the cities where public transportation systems have provided both bus service and other mass transportation systems services, the results are basically the same. The nation's transit companies, which operated at $149 million profit at the end of World War II, incurred an aggregate deficit of about $300 million in 1971. About one-half of this deficit originates in New York, Chicago, Boston, Philadelphia, Cleveland, and San Francisco, where cities operate rail transit systems as well as providing bus service. But the remainder of the deficit comes from about one thousand communities in the United States that provide only bus service.

Although about two and one half million people daily ride the subways, buses, and railroads within the New York City metropolitan area, the New York Metropolitan Area Transportation companies had an aggregate deficit of about $115 million at the start of the 1970 decade. It is expected that that deficit will continue to rise. For example, the estimates of the cost of providing each subway trip in New York City averaged about 47 cents while each customer paid about an average of 30 cents. The average cost of the average subway ride is expected to rise to 78 cents by 1974. The current average cost revenue ratio has produced an annual deficit for the Long Island Railroad of about 10 million dollars per year and about one million dollars per month for the Port Authority Trans-Hudson (PATH) system.

Despite the almost overwhelming problems of maintaining adequate mass transportation systems as well as an adequate intraurban expressway system, transportation capacity in most urban areas for most individuals has improved during the last decade. The exceptions to the transportation capacity increase are keyed to congestion and to the transportation capacity improvements unequally distributed among residents in urban areas. For example, low-income families have become worse off, particularly elderly people who have low and fixed incomes and who do not own or drive automobiles. The real income of the poor and nondriving old has been significantly reduced as a direct function of the increasing family income and increasing automobile ownership of nonpoor urban residents. The ownership of more than one car by affluent families magnifies the impact. With additional automobile transport available, decreasing demand has weakened the economic position of the mass transportation systems and has brought about a decline and frequency of service.

Public policies, which have allocated disproportionately large funding for highway and automobile related transport, have not benefited low-income urban families. Although almost all families in the United States earning $10,000 or more have, at least, one car, only 50% of the poverty-level families own or operate an automobile. Even in the city of Detroit, 27% of all families and 60% of all inner-city families cannot afford to buy or operate an automobile.

II. DEMAND FOR TRANSPORTATION

The demand for all varieties of urban transportation is inter-related. Highway use and the resulting highway traffic congestion at peak use affects the efficiency of the use of other surface and subsurface modes of transport. The automobiles and highways dominate the urban transportation problems simply because nearly 70% of all transportation trips in urban areas are in automobiles. But the nature and the type of transportation facilities offered in any urban area is a function of a variety of factors some of which may be particularly localized in selected urban areas. Each city differs in its physical and economic characteristics, income level and distribution, and in a variety of other factors. These differentials account for varieties as to the type and quality of transportation modes and facilities needed to provide the mobility of resources in urban areas.

Studies by Karl Moskowitz assumed that individuals selecting alternative modes of transportation are attempting to maximize satisfaction or maximize utility from the use of the transportation mode or method. Each person using alternative transportation has made a choice between various modes of travel or combinations of transportation means. The traveler in making the choice attempts to maximize satisfaction and minimize the discomfort involved in making any particular trip. His specific decision will be a function of the syndrome of economic and personal factors that are relevant to his particular needs, and that reflect in the demand for transportation services. There are extensive factors that affect the decision, but certain characteristics are usually considered to have the heaviest weight or to be the most significant, that is, "the essential characteristics of various modes facing the commuter are the money costs, the time in route, and the various physiological and physical attributes of the mode which can be called the disutility involved in the traveling by that mode. . . . while one person may spend a great deal just to save a few minutes, another will take a slower or more expensive mode because he can't stand traveling on a

---

[1] Karl Moskowitz, "Living and Traveling Patterns in Automobile Oriented Cities," Reproduced in George M. Smerk, *Readings in Urban Transporta-*

seemingly superior alternative."[1] Most Americans living in urban areas are faced with this transportation decision on a daily basis and the decision is associated with the journey to work. That journey-to-work choice and the demand for alternative transportation modes is reflected and is additive to "peak demand for transportation modes." The following sections review the now traditional approaches to peak demand for transportation facilities.

III. THE JOURNEY TO WORK

A person traveling to work with the option of various modes can evaluate his equivalents of marginal value of leisure and travel in terms of alternative modes and costs of transportation. The trade-off between travel and other time use is a factor in determining place of employment and residence. The income earned by an urban resident is related to his job and location of employment. If it is assumed that all residents attempt to maximize utility from earned income, a series of trade-offs occurs between conditions that increase utility and conditions in his life style that decrease utility. The cost of earning income is a cost that offsets increases in utilities from the spending of income. Money and real or psychic costs are involved in resident location relative to location of income at place of employment. Money costs include the land and a unique element of rent of land determined by the distances from the place of work to place of residence. In addition to the time cost, the worker makes money outlays for transportation that are included in the calculation for various locations of employment and residence. Money costs vary with the mode of transportation. Given total cost of alternate transportation, costs are chargeable "against the gross returns from the worker's employment, and may be treated in a somewhat similar fashion with time costs."[2]

Time or psychic costs, plus money costs ultimately appear in an employer's total input cost as a type of imputed travel cost.[3]

---

tion (Bloomington, Indiana, University of Indiana Press, 1968), pp. 164–166.

[2] Wingo, op. cit., p. 60.

[3] See Wingo, op. cit., Chapter III, pp. 52–62.

Studies[4] of journey-to-work patterns and distances as a determinant in residential location choice indicate that households are located at varying distances from work because of transportation costs, preference for locations, and incomes. Using Detroit as an example with land distributed among manufacturing or industrial and residential uses, workers employed in high income occupations and working near the central business district (CBD) tended to make longer journeys to work and to reside in the suburbs. When employed in the suburbs, workers made shorter journeys to work from their nearby housing. Lower income workers made short journeys to work and resided close to their work regardless of the location of the work place.[5]

Effective demand for commuter types of transit and new suburban housing are complementary. Public policies that help to promote the demand for one of these goods will also increase effective demand for the other.[6] This demand interrelationship is important particularly for central city residents whose effective demand for suburban new housing is limited. Where the effective demand for new housing and commuter transit has been influential in the design of urban transport services, the inner-city resident has been increasingly disadvantaged by limited access to low time and money cost "journey-to-work" or to "job-access" transit facilities.

A. *Peak Demand*

There are two peak demand periods during any given day, that is, in the morning, home to work, and, in the evening, work to home. Transportation facilities are also required for social and recreational travel and for a polyglot of other trips that are associated with shopping, visits, and taking the children to school.

---

[4] John F. Kain, "The Journey to Work as a Determinant of Residential Location," loc. cit.

[5] Ibid., p. 225. Also see John F. Kain, "Housing Segregation, Negro Employment, in Metropolitan De-Centralization," Program on Regional and Urban Economics, Discussion Paper No. 14, MIT-Harvard Joint Study on Urban Studies, July 1967 (revised) mimeographed, pp. 2–5.

[6] See J. B. Meyer, J. F. Kain, and M. Wohl, *The Urban Transport Problem* (Cambridge: Harvard University Press, 1965), p. 362.

Social and recreational trips occur typically on weekends and usually involve auto transportation. Given the use requirements, transport facilities must be designed to accommodate the peak-hour trips. Demand for transportation services can be specified as to the number of units of output consumed at different levels of cost. Demand as a concept can be expressed as the demand for movement, the traffic demand, flow demand, and deadline demand.[7]

B. Demand Concepts

Traffic demand is a reference to frequency and routes of trips. Flow demand can be associated with the number of traffic units that flow passed a specific place at a given time. Reference to the specific destination or terminal place, by frequency of trips or patterns of trips, identifies deadline demand. A different concept of demand oriented toward the pattern of frequency or total trips that people take or want to take, is termed the demand for movement.

Among the different types of demand for transportation services, the patterns of movement for various purposes reflects regularity simply because certain trips are more systematic in terms of time and space use. The most important is the journey to work.

. . . The journey-to-work problem has the lowest "price elasticity" of demand of all other classes: it would take a very large change in the cost of the work trip to have a perceptible effect on the number of personal trips in the short run. In the aggregate, the journey-to-work has a higher degree of order than the other classes of movement because of the manner in which work is institutionalized in the community. The other classes of movement relate to the activities whose location tends to be dependent on the distribution of households or to situations in which the household has a considerable number of alternatives as to where and when its transactions may be carried out. Finally, the rigorous time constraints of the journey-to-work are responsible for the massible "peaking" in the urban

---

[7] Ibid., p. 28.

areas—and, hence, the low load factor—of the demand for transportation services.[8]

The most significant "trip purpose" in highway transportation demand is the journey to work and places periodic pressure on the available supply of transport services.

III. TRANSPORTATION SUPPLY OR CAPACITY

Although there are a variety of forms of transportation demand, *short-run* supply of transport services is simply a reference to the physical plant and equipment available for movement at any given time. Another but less important concept of supply refers to the different opportunities for movement between selected points or locations at specified times.

One researcher has identified and developed, at least, two capacity or supply definitions. The first suggests that "for any given speed a flow capacity is reached when no space in the flow is wasted, a condition designated 'velocity-specific capacity.'" The second characteristic of distinguishing capacity is "system capacity which is the maximum 'velocity-specific capacity of all speeds of flow, and the velocity at which it is reached.'"[9]

Capacity in a uniform flow system is determined by the velocity at which the carriers move and the distance between them. It follows that if they could move in a system so that the interval between them were independent of their velocity, the volume handled by the system could be increased by an increase in the system's velocity, and the capacity would be limited only by the technological limits to the velocity of the carriers. In reality, however, where each unit is controlled independently, as in the case of automobile traffic, the interval between carriers is the 'safety factor' necessary to avoid collision and interruption of flow and is directly related to the time required for a carrier to accommodate its behavior to that of the carrier ahead.

---

[8] Lowden Wingo, Jr., *Transportation and Urban Land* (Baltimore: Johns Hopkins Press, Resources for the Future, Inc., 1961), p. 35.
[9] Lowden Wingo, Jr., *Technology in Urban Transportation Systems*, op. cit., p. 38.

If this time is constant, the distance between units related directly to their velocity, and the amount of space in the moving stream of traffic required by unit will vary with the velocity of the flow. Consequently, the number of units that can be accommodated per unit at a time, that is, the capacity of the system depends directly on the flow of velocity.[10]

Transportation supply is synonymous with transportation capacity.

IV. DEMAND, SUPPLY, AND PRICE DETERMINATION

In a functioning market system, if the supply price of goods or a service is below an equilibrium price, excess demand occurs. With transportation facilities, existing prices of transportation service produce excess demand or congestion. Traffic tie-ups are evidences of excess motor vehicle demand. Current pricing arrangements are not effective, since they do not equate the supply of road space (for the automobile) with demand. Congestion becomes a predominant method of allocating space for too many vehicles using the same highway at the same time. In other words, if the peak capacity of the highway system is not great enough, capacity tends to be reduced when the need for the facility is the greatest.

Congestion is the single most important factor limiting the improvement of bus transportation on metropolitan expressways and highways.

A. Congestion as a Pricing Problem

General congestion as opposed to bottleneck congestion suggests that demand for highway or other transportation space actually exceeds the supply at given prices. "If prices are higher than costs, the basic difficulty is in short supply. If costs are higher than prices, the basic difficulty is in excess demand resulting from underpricing. Urban transportation has been affected by both situations."[11]

The allocation of the revenue from highway uses has tended

---

[10] Ibid., pp. 37–38.
[11] Lyle C. Fitch and Associates, *Urban Transportation and Public Policy* (San Francisco, Chandler Publishing Co., 1964), p. 129.

to amplify the "short supply" characteristics of urban roads. A considerable proportion of revenue produced by motor vehicle use in cities is and, historically, has been allocated for services in rural areas. The effects of this diversion of revenues are (1) the reduction of the supply and quality of roads in urban areas and (2) the requirement that cities finance highway and street expenditures from nonhighway sources.[12]

In the high density areas of large urban regions, however, it appears that part of the difficulty lies in underpricing of highway travel relative to the cost, that is, user charges do not cover direct and indirect costs of highway use, and consequently travel in high density areas tends to be heavily subsidized.[13]

Congestion on freeways indicates an absence of pricing arrangements for users of mobility facilities. Since the price mechanism is faulty, there is malallocation of resources. The allocation problem is persistent, since there is no way of reducing congestion as long as excess demand persists. It is also difficult to determine future or latent demand for mobility. There is no assurance that more freeway construction will reduce congestion on the new highways. The malallocation is symbolic evidence that pricing systems have not been adequately tested as a means of equating supply and demand. With no equilibrium pricing levels there are no adequate criteria for determining the capacity or highway investment. A long run, nonoptimal solution is continuous investment in highways to insure free-flowing movement between all points at all times.

Lyle C. Fitch recommended a series of charges for driving. This pricing solution must be consistent with the cost-price of freeway and highway use, and must fluctuate with the level of demand for the facilities. Higher prices should be charged during peak demand and lower prices set and levied for off-peak-hours use. This is analogous to electric rates with differentials to discriminate against users in peak and off-peak periods. The use of the private automobile is the most important factor in the inability of highways and highways systems and expressways to reflect a price system regulatory mechanism.

---

[12] Ibid.
[13] Ibid.

Our present system of user charges or the pricing of highways is principally the federal and state excise taxes charged on motor-vehicle fuels. Fuel taxes are proportional, that is, x number of cents per gallon of fuel. This user price is an average for all conditions of road use and does not discriminate for the high- and low-cost roads, or travel at peak or at nonpeak hours. The only variation introduced in user cost is related to the different consumption rates of motor-vehicle fuel.

The difficulty with the present system of averaging charges is that it frequently involves heavy subsidies to a particular segment of a particular type of trip—the peak hour trip into or through congestion prone urban centers—when there are alternatives open to some classes of uses: (1) the use of alternative transportation modes or combinations of modes such as park-and-ride arrangements, (2) alternative routes, (3) shifting to off-peak hours, and (4) different linkages between origin and destination as in the linkage of home-to-job.[14]

But federal policies have played a significant role in the causal factors that make urban transport use high-cost and low-benefit activities for urban residents. Federal policies have been established and implemented to exclude the possibility of appropriate pricing or cost of transport facilities. Transportation facilities, their construction and financing, generate a variety of user and nonuser costs. Most of these costs are not compensated for in federal programs nor are charged against highway use.

B. Costs of Construction

Highway design alters the relative accessibility of the various sections of a city. Highways must be built at or near ground level and thus through or around existing uses of sites. This statement is profound only to the extent that highways under construction and in use incur both costs and benefits to users and nonusers. Highway construction alters land values, either by increasing the values of land that are newly accessible, near major interchanges, or by reducing land values for locations near an older highway with a reduced volume of traffic. Other costs, in addition to the reduction in values in urban areas, are

---

[14] Ibid., p. 139.

constant noise, air pollution, glare, and bottlenecks on local access streets near interchanges.

Many federally financed highways impose other significant uncompensated costs. Anthony Downs has documented some of them:

(1) disruption of traffic flows and accessibility of specific commercial or residential areas, or noise and vibrations, during periods of construction imposes serious costs on local merchants and industrial firms, but they receive no compensation; (2) moving costs are grossly undercompensated, especially for large establishments and estates where compensation limits exist; (3) many small businesses are forced to liquidate because they are cut off from their market or compelled to move away from their established clientele, or forced to leave low rent quarters and move to high rent quarters they cannot afford.

. . . 237,000 displaced persons and another 230,000 nondisplaced persons per year will be affected. This amounts to a potential noncompensated loss from $812 to $1194 per household affected—or from 20 to 30% of the average household income of those concerned. If the government paid the full cost involved, this would add 14 to 20% to the total cost requiring all real property concerned. *Hence the magnitude of the injustices arising from such narrowness of viewpoint—is hardly trivial. Rather, it is large.* I believe that the figures from this one form of injustice alone are persuasive evidence that more comprehensive economic analysis are necessary for proper assessment—and executive—of proposed federal urban projects.[15]

Poor land use and transportation planning has also contributed to the efficiency and development of alternative and competitive transportation modes. Local and federal urban planning and transit planning are in large measure responsible for the maldistribution in transportation facilities available in urban areas. Historically, planning studies of transportation problems have concentrated on only selected forms of transportation instead

---

[15] Anthony Downs, "Some Aspects of the Proper Use of Economic Analysis in Federal Urban Programs," *Economic Analysis and Efficiency in Government,* Hearings before the Subcommittee on Economy in Government of the Joint Economic Committee, Congress of the United States, 91st Congress, First Session, Part 2, September 22, 23, and 24, 1969. Washington, D.C., 1970, p. 285.

of on a comprehensive planning for all transportation. Planners are subject to criticism because transportation planning is ordinarily not coordinated with other development or land-use planning. Now and in the past, there is no agreement among urban transportation experts as to what is an ideal urban transportation design. There is no concensus as to the urban configuration that is ideal vis-à-vis a transportation system.[16]

Government action in transport has introduced strong misallocation effects in past highway construction policies. The federal government's policy actions in urban transportation are subject to extensive criticism on allocative grounds. The federal government spent approximately $5 billion on new highway construction in 1969 but less than $200 million for public transportation services such as subways and buses. The federal government defrays approximately 90% of the building costs of new highway construction but applies different funding and lower subsidies for alternative mass transportation. The total federal moneys spent on urban public transportation since 1965 is equal to the amount spent on federal urban highway programs in the 6-month period January 1 to July 31, 1970. The current pattern of federal spending emphasis on highway construction is symbolic of this historical distortion in United States transportation policy (see Table 7-1).

V. FEDERAL TRANSPORT POLICY

Post-World War II federal support for highway transportation was expanded in 1956 under the Federal Aid Highway Act. This 1956 legislation provided for federal financing for "a transportation system." Because of the way in which the program was structured, federal support for "transportation" became a program for highway construction.

The Federal Aid Highway Act of 1956 provided funds for greatly accelerated highway building. This Act initially authorized expenditures of about $42 billion over a 13-year period for highway construction. Twenty-five of the $42 billion was allo-

---

[16] J. R. Meyer, J. F. Kain, M. Wohl, *The Urban Transportation Problem,* op. cit., pp. 365–366.

Table 7-1. Federal Budget Outlays for Transportation by Agency or Program, Selected Fiscal Years 1955 to 1972 (Millions of Dollars)

Agency or Program	1955	1960	1965	1970	1972
Department of Transportation					
Highway	636	2,978	4,069	4,507	4,923
Aviation	122	508	756	1,223	1,834
Railroad	2	3	3	17	57
Coast Guard	190	238	367	588	661
Urban mass transit	0	0	11	106	327
Other	0	0	23	− 8	22
Offsetting receipts	0	0	−20	−16	−19
Subtotal	950	3,727	5,209	6,417	7,805
Other Agencies	342	539	818	715	986
Total	1,292	4,266	6,027	7,168	8,791

Source. Setting National Priorities, The 1972 Budget, Brookings Institution, Washington D.C., p. 260.

cated for the construction of a national system of interstate highways. The federal government provided 90% of the cost of the interstate's construction, and the states in which the system was developed contributed only 10%.[17] When the 1956 Highway Act was passed, Lewis Mumford was reported to have said "the most charitable thing to assume about this action is that they hadn't the faintest notion of what they were doing." In retrospect this statement by Mumford anticipated the impact of the highway program on urban problems. The Highway Act of 1956 set a mileage limitation of the interstate system at 41,000 miles. It also established special provisions for the financing of the interstate system and federal aid highways. The interstate system was scheduled to be completed in 1972. The total cost for the system is estimated to be about $47 billion. At the beginning of this decade about two-thirds of the mileage had been completed at a cost of more than $30 billion.

A. Effects of Transport Policies

The design and methods of allocation of resources for highway construction under the 1956 act have encouraged and fostered

---

[17] D. Philip Locklin, *Economics of Transportation* (Homewood, Illinois. Richard D. Irwin, Inc., 6th edition, 1966), p. 629.

urban sprawl. The supply of urban and interurban highways was determined by federal and state government officials and was influenced by industries that benefited from the existence of the construction of the freeway system. The demand for the use of highway facilities was generated by the public and private sector, or for the users of trucks and automobiles. With the method of financing, demand is a reflection of consumer preferences for a "free good."

The method of financing the highway network under the federal program specified that Congress pay about 90% of the cost of building interstate freeways. The source of revenues for the federal portion of the cost was from the federal gasoline excise tax.

A supply-and-demand mechanism has not been operative to produce price or cost rationing of facilities provided under the Highway Act of 1956. By the beginning of the 1970s the federal government had made cumulative errors in its decision to encourage the use of automobiles for urban mobility needs. Mobility requirements for the central city area are best served by nonautomobile modes. The freeways and interurban highways were basically designed to make central city areas more accessible to suburbanites. The Highway Act of 1956 has increased the flow of cars into the center city and out of the center city areas during peak periods and has produced bottlenecks and general congestion plus increases in air pollution. There has also been a related increase in central-city land use areas for parking lots, garages, and facilities designed for the automobile. The increase in automobile-related land use has displaced people and businesses in central cities. Increased highway construction designed to improve inner city access has, in fact, resulted in fewer people traveling to the central city business districts than before the freeways were built.

During the first five years of the administration of the Highway Act, the federal government had no significant program for financing or developing urban transportation systems. Until the beginning of the 1970 decade, there was no evidence that the federal government was vitally interested in directing economic resources into nonhighway urban transportation programs or to reallocate resources via an effective market mechanism into other transportation modes.

Token federal programs in mass transportation were begun in 1961. These programs were introduced largely as a result of railroad passenger deficits. In 1961 under a Housing and Urban Development Act, emergency loan monies were provided for demonstration grants for mass transit. In 1964 after experiences of inadequate and ineffective activity, the federal government provided federal matching grants for the preservation and improvement of mass transportation systems. A research and development program authorized in the 1964 Urban Mass Transportation Act was amended and expanded in 1966, but only minimal financing was made available.

The Mass Tranportation Act of 1968 reflected the growing federal concern for the need to develop a transportation system. The Department of Transportation was established under the act as an autonomous agency responsible for all transportation programs. The reorganization was (a) to facilitate the development of urban transportation, (b) to foster a desirable planning for urban development, (c) to improve the movement of goods and people in cities, and (d) to provide compatibility with regional and national transportation networks. But from the end of World War II to 1965, public transportation suffered increasingly larger operating deficits. During that period fares for mass transportation increased about 300% while revenue passenger miles declined about two-thirds. Mass transportation companies rapidly disappeared as a result of bankruptcy, abandonment, and absorption into other companies. More than 120 mass transportation companies have disappeared since 1945, and 70 of these were in cities of less than 25,000 population. There are approximately 90 additional companies currently experiencing financial difficulty. Despite the increasing number of failures of bus systems in small towns, the bus has emerged as the predominant vehicle for surface public transportation. Of the three types of surface carriers (bus, streetcar, and trolley coach), the bus is the only mode that remains a viable alternative. The last streetcar was delivered to a transit company in 1952, and the last trolley coach in 1955. There is no future use of trolley coach anticipated after the existing equipment is depreciated or has ended its service life. Surface transportation systems, primarily buses, carry about 75% of all mass transit passengers. The remaining 25% are carried by rail rapid-transit or by other means.

A report on national transportation policy called the Doyle report,[18] produced in the early part of the 1960s, examined problems of commuter services particularly for railroads in large urban areas such as New York, Chicago, Boston, and Philadelphia. Its conclusions indicated that rail commuting services were not costed out in such a way as to cover the deficits for passenger transportation, and such deficits were being made up from freed revenues. The pattern of continuing losses from suburban transportation passenger services had forced the railroads to stop much of their train service, which is in direct conflict with the needs of commuters for improved transportation. But the report pointed out that suburban rail commuter service was primarily a local city problem and that the major efforts to continue the service ought to be undertaken by local authorities. The Doyle report stated that the most important forces affecting the urban rail services were external to the railroad and mainly beyond the control of the local company managers.[19]

It is generally conceded that rail rapid-transit systems are feasible only in very large urban areas with high population densities. The majority of cities will continue to rely on bus transportation. The subway is an efficient means of moving large numbers of passengers in high density urban areas, but the subway is inflexible and expensive. Because of the expense of separate rights of way, only extremely dense population and employment centers can effectively utilize subways. The relative efficiency and effectiveness of alternative transportation modes now appear to be a problem of interest to federal transporta-

---

[18] The Doyle Report: "National Transportation Policy, Preliminary Draft of a Report to the Senate Committee on Interstate and Foreign Commerce, 87th Congress, 1st Session, Washington, D.C., United States Government Printing Office, 1961. The report carried no analysis of the overall urban or metropolitan transportation problem.

[19] Dudley F. Pengrum, *Transportation Economics and Public Policy* (Homewood, Illinois, Richard D. Irwin, Inc., revised edition, 1968), p. 602.

tion experts. That interest is reflected in the design of the Transportation Act of 1968.

B. New Emphasis in Transport Policy

The federal government's current program in urban transportation was designed to develop a "balanced transportation system."

The announced basic objective of the federal Department of Transportation is to promote "greater comfort, safety, speed, efficiency, and reliability in all modes of transportation." The proposed expenditures for the department of transportation during fiscal year 1971 reflects an increase in emphasis in urban transportation.[20] The allocation of funds indicates that while funds for highways continue to exceed those for other forms of transportation, the emphasis on urban mass transit and air transport is increasing relative to highways and water. Current programs call for an allocation of $10 billion in grants and aids for a 12-year period (1971 to 1982). Funds, when appropriated, will be allocated to cities of all sizes in amounts to cover about two-thirds of the cost of development and construction of new rail systems; and of installing modern communications equipment. Financial assistance may be made available to private transportation operators to purchase new equipment and to improve service. Private operators will be required to meet the planning standards of local regulatory bodies and to make assurances that federal funds will be spent for transportation purposes.

Under this legislation, federal assistance will be available to buy land or rights of way to be used for transportation systems. In cases where the transportation investment has a substantial impact on the community, the local government is required to hold public hearings as a form of community participation in the decision-making process.

This proposed development of the balanced transportation system also provides federal funds to conduct research to develop better means of providing urban transportation facilities.

The proposed federal program is broad in scope and includes

---

[20] See Special Analyses, Budget of the United States, Fiscal Year 1971, Washington, D.C., United States Government Printing Office, 1970, p. 285.

(a) assistance for capital improvements, (b) subsidized research and technology in public transportation, (c) assurances to state and local governments that the federal government will carry out long-range plans and will meet the rising costs of transportation needs, (d) encouragement that bus riders, train commuters, and subway users will get better service, and (e) possibilities that the automobile driver may be able to travel on less-congested roads. There is, however, no uniform positive assessment of the capacity of the federal government's program to have meaningful impact on the urban transportation problems.

The federal program must rely on funds appropriated by Congress to fund its proposals. This is a sharp departure from the methods of financing for the support of highways. Instead of establishing a trust fund similar to the highway trust fund, transit program funding will rely on regular congressional appropriations that are made to carry out the long-term proposals under this program. There are no earmarked sources of money comparable to gasoline taxes to assure a flow of revenue to fund the program, even if the program itself is adequate.

The major future issue in modern urban transportation will be the same as the current issue—the continuing controversy about the volume of new investment in highways relative to the needed improvements in public transportation facilities.

VI. THE AUTOMOBILE—PREFERRED TRANSPORT

Consumer preferences should play a role in establishing solutions-oriented policies for urban transportation problems. The private automobile is the significant factor in the pattern of consumer preferences for transportation facilities. Consumer preferences for automobiles suggest that appropriate economic policies must change (a) the cost of use of the automobile, (b) the cost of parking automobiles in cities, or (c) burdensome money outlays for parking, travel time, and access to highways should be introduced into the decision-making patterns of individuals who use automobiles. In the future, as income increases with increased economic growth, the automobile will continue to be used by more urban residents. Any solution to urban transportation problems will be an automobile-related solution. Alternatives should be designed to eliminate the automobile or to make travel by automobile less undesirable.

The cost-price impact in allocating consumer preferences provides a general orientation for dealing with the problem of urban transportation. Programs should increase the supply of facilities for automobiles or should reduce the level of demand for facilities by private automobile users. If the market is allowed to determine equilibrium prices, other transport market-related indicators should provide guidelines for policy makers.

Nonprivate automobile users of highway facilities in urban areas operate in a unique market structure. Bus transportation and taxis are substitutes for the private automobile. Taxis must be licensed and buses must be franchised. Both the licensing and franchise devices limit the supply of transportation services. The substitution effect between automobiles and taxis is limited by the number of taxis permitted to be licensed. An increase in substitution could be achieved by permitting the market to operate to determine the number of taxis on streets. It is assumed that there would be appropriate safety and maintenance controls to insure the quality of service for taxi riders, but the market would determine the number of taxis needed in urban areas. More freedom of operation in setting rates of return and charges on bus routes or facilities might be helpful in reallocating urban transportation facilities. Buses, if permitted to operate with more flexibility in routes and frequency, may provide transportation that would be used in larger amounts by urban residents. It is unfortunate that the federal mass transportation program started prior to the testing of free market action in determining the resources needed for bus facilities.

Given the history of our noncoordinated transport policies, the absence of price influences in the choice of automobile use, the high cost of construction of separate rights of way for buses, and the deterioration of mass transit facilities, the effect has been to increase the use of automobile travel and highway investment, and thus drive travelers away from bus and rail transport. The transportation problem in cities is the coordination of, or efficient allocation of, highway physical plant.

VII. MAKING THE MARKET WORK

The reallocation of existing plant and facilities is an appropriate
way to reduce the incidence and variety of urban transportation
problems.

There are rationing processes that can be used to alleviate congestion problems. User costs or tolls should be charged to reflect
higher costs of use during peak-load periods. The tolls or user
charges should be based on differentials or discriminatory pricing
patterns. Commuters using the highway system should pay a
higher price than individuals using the same facility during a
lower-load period. Lower fares for mass transit should be adopted
to increase the cost differentials between automobile and nonautomobile travel. Tunnel and bridge tolls should also aid in
rationing facilities to the advantage of high-volume vehicles. Differential tolls would ration transport facilities and would bring
about the improved coordination of the various modes through
the cross-elasticity of demand for transport services. Another rationing device that should be used is highway flow control.
Controls for access could be implemented so the flow of cars and
buses onto the highway would be limited. A series of gates or
barriers at bottleneck locations would limit highway use.[21]

A type of rationing, monitoring, and priority system for buses
has been used in Milwaukee, Seattle, and Washington, D. C.
Express buses that use a separate lane of the interstate highway
from northern Virginia has been tested on an experimental basis.
Only buses are allowed to use a selected lane of the highway.
This permits buses to maintain high speeds and to quickly travel
the distances from the low-density land use areas of suburban
"bedroom communities" into the traffic bottlenecks of Washington, D. C.

. . . A sophisticated manipulation of tolls, parking charges, licenses,
and other user charges by the urban transportation authority would
tend to promote or penalize a given activity or land use pattern. By
altering the relative transportation price structure that bears on job
commuters, shoppers, and others as they move short or long distances

---

[21] See the analysis of Meyer, Kain, and Wohl, op. cit., Chapter 14.

at on- or off-peak hours and stay short or long periods at various sites, the public transportation authority could exert a significant, if not major force on the form and function of the community.[22]

If such private-public economic rationing is done well, market forces will determine price-cost relationships and other variables for all modes of transportation. If the market were to indicate comparative costs for each mode of transportation or could identify demand and supply relationships, equilibrium prices could be established for each of the types of transportation services. The relationship between public and private interests and responsibilities as well as economic activities associated with each type of transportation system needs to be more effectively coordinated through the implementation of a more freely operating and, perhaps, autonomous market environment for intraurban transportation facilities.

VIII. ALTERNATIVES TO MARKET-RELATED POLICIES

Even if public-private economic rationing is implemented effectively and market forces determine price-cost relationships and other variables for all modes of transportation, urban residents who are excluded from participating in markets because of low income, job access, and for other reasons will not benefit from improved market functioning as a method to deal with urban transportation efficiency. For many inner-city residents, private and public transportation is not accessible. For many other urban residents the time costs attributed to traveling on existing means with many transfers and long trips to suburban factories or job sites make job access difficult or impossible. The current and rising costs of fares are too high for other urban potential users of the transportation system. Still other inner-city residents with extremely low educational attainment, particularly reading skills, find that the complexity of instructions and directions precludes their use of transportation systems in the city.

Urban transportation access and use is a major difficulty in

---

22 Wilbur R. Thompson, *A Preface to Urban Economics* (Baltimore: Johns Hopkins Press, published for the Resources for the Future, Inc., 1968), p. 349.

making jobs accessible to the central-city unemployed. Improvement in the transportation system is a unique promising technique for the attainment of economic progress through mobility for the inner-city unemployed and underemployed. Cities with underdeveloped central cores need to evaluate programs for expanding and improving public urban transportation. This improvement should be oriented toward providing direct access or transportation lines between job opportunities in the central city and reducing the number of transfers necessary to reach any employment center in the city and toward making transportation faster and designing a rational pattern of subsidy of transportation facilities to reduce fares for inner-city workers. The money cost of implementing subsidized or free transit between the central city and suburban job opportunities will, of course, be high. But relative to the cost of ghetto industrial development programs, tax subsidies, or other incentives for industries locating in central-city areas, transport costs are quite low.

A variety of other factors that include increasing urban size, congestion, pollution, and simply too many automobiles make improved transit systems necessary in most urban areas at some time in the near future. The improved transportation linkage between inner-city residents and adjacent areas is a first-ranking priority in improved metropolitan transportation systems.

IX. FUTURE POLICIES

Elimination or manageability of urban transportation problems requires both micro- and macro-policy implementation. Most important is the coordination of a variety of policies that recognize the distinct interrelationship of resource investment in all transportation modes. The rapid improvement in the road systems without an accompanying development of mass transportation systems has made automobile traffic congestion worse. The heavy resource commitment by the federal government for road improvement, particularly urban expressways, without a commitment to similar programs for other forms of urban commuter transit has resulted in higher peak-hour automobile congestion even in cities that have a fairly well-established mass transportation system. Micro-policies would assure that the charging of tolls on urban expressways and that other forms of rationing automobile vehicular use at peak periods must be accompanied by a subsidy of particular users in order to develop a balanced and effective transportation system. Macro policies would assure that such unifying and coordinating policies for urban transportation systems are components of comprehensive urban development programs.

8

Urban Housing—Problems and Policy

A. Location, Land Use, and Economic Behavior

Spatial distribution processes determine the use of certain locations of urban space for housing sites vis-à-vis other land-use activities. Housing decisions are made with reference to transportation facilities that make employment and other locational advantages available to a residential location.

In terms of economic behavior each householder as well as each employer attempts to select the optimum location from all choices available. The spatial distribution, pattern, or urban economic activity is a function of an "optimality" orientation, or the application of, equilibrium theory to housing decisions.

B. Choosing Residential Locations

Homeowners try to choose residential locations or use land for residential space in much the same way that they allocate income for other economic goods. The purchase of residential locations or residential space use is one of the series of decisions made in income allocations as homeowners attempt to maximize utility. The quantity of residential land use that the householder will buy depends on income, the price of residential land, and the preference pattern for location.

C. Demand for Housing

In determining private demand for residential housing, house design, floor plan, and location in particular sections of the city on given streets are functions of preference of the consumer and the availability of construction resources. In the post-World War II development of residential construction in the United States, people in suburbs have demanded single-family dwellings, while central-city and near central-city construction has been dominated by apartment/condominium living arrangements.

As in the case of any other consumer goods, the asset and money income position of the individual home buyer is a constraint. Since housing represents the largest single expenditure of the average American, income or the ability to finance the house is dominant in private demand patterns. Individuals buying housing seldom pay cash. Typical home consumers buy credit from local commercial banks that are willing to handle real estate financing. If the potential homeowner borrows from a commerical bank or savings and loan institution, he must have a cash down payment from about 25% to 33% of the purchase price.[1]

The availability of credit and the cost of borrowing, or interest rate, directly affects the private demand for residential housing. Thus demand for housing is predicated on a variety of factors, which incorporate many of the characteristics of personal behavior attributable to rational buyers in microeconomic theory. Given demand forces interacting with supply forces will determine price and output for the residential construction industry.

D. Housing Supply and Cost of Production

The American housing industry is made up of a large number of small contractors and builders and a small number of large

---

[1] Certain savings and loan institutions in the United States have been used by the federal government as the principal means to make mortgage credit available for potential homeowners. The Federal National Mortgage Association and the Government National Mortgage Association are ready buyers and make the market for mortgage paper. These practices assure liquidity for savings and loan institutions. Commercial banks are also aided by the federal government in mortgage financing by insuring loans under Federal Housing Administration and Veterans Administration legislation. Under the Housing Act of 1968 and the Model Cities Programs, the federal government may provide subsidies to low-income homeowners and make credit available at low interest costs.

national construction firms. In the microeconomics sense, this market may be characterized as atomistic in structure. The atomistic reference is to the fact that the industry is composed of many small producers, builders, or contractors who represent the total productive capacity of the industry.

When contracting for a house, the home buyer finds that his builder or contractor may have a few carpenters or a few bricklayers working on salary, but most of the work in the construction sequence of the house is subcontracted to other dealers. The foundation is let to one firm, while the plumbing is contracted to another dealer. The furnace and heating would be subcontracted, as would the roofing and, perhaps, the interior finishing. Thus even though the contractor is a builder, in effect, he is an organizer of production in the traditional entrepreneurial sense.

One of the distinguishing characteristics of residential housing is that the supply has basically local impact and the market for such housing is localized. The building materials used in the housing industry are sunk costs which, once committed to a given residential site, are immobile thereafter. The immobility factor creates situations in which there may be gluts in some housing markets and, at the same time, shortages in other markets because of unique local characteristics.

As a result of the localized nature of the housing market as well as the diversity in climate, features, and preference of style, the costs of construction of houses vary throughout the United States. In almost all areas, however, data indicate that one input factor, labor, accounts for more than one-half of the total cost of any residential unit.

But many factors account for the pattern of total cost changes in the housing industry. Housing construction costs in the United States during the late 1960s rose about 7.5% per year. The principal factor in the cost rises was the increase in the average hourly wages for the building-trades craftsmen. Wages for these building craftsmen have risen more per year than the price of materials. The basic hourly wage rates at the end of the 1960 decade were 430% of the 1941 level. Materials prices were 240%, compared to the 1941 level. Total construction costs for builders and investors are about 220% higher than in 1941.

Housing costs have increased partly because of and despite

high profits and improvements in the quality of housing construction. The evidence of inflation and, perhaps, quality changes in single-family dwellings is reflected in costs figures. For example, in 1962 the average one-family home sold for $17,500; by 1966 this figure was $22,200, and had increased to about $25,000 by the end of the 1960 decade.

A major factor in total cost was labor cost and the methods of construction. Innovative attempts to mass produce low-cost housing have resulted in construction costs of about $18 a square foot for single homes and $15 a square foot for apartments on "factory" produced houses in 1969. One manufacturer of an 800-unit complex in Detroit was able to build town houses at $11.50 per square foot excluding land, or 25% cheaper than similar conventional built houses. For these "low-cost" units under current subsidies, rent would be $98 a month for a one-bedroom apartment and $158 for a four-bedroom apartment. Without rent subsidies, the apartment rent would range from $125 to $185 on the nonprofit basis.[2]

Inflation has been responsible for dramatic increases in material and construction costs, land values, and rental prices. The indexes of construction costs rose 6% in 1967, increased at an annual rate of 7% in 1968, and further increased to a 10% annual rate by 1970. Land prices have experienced a similar rise during the 1960s. By 1970, land was more than 22% of the total cost of a single-family home (up 12% since 1950). Continuing increases in land prices or land costs bring changes in quality and style of housing simply because contractors "cut corners" or seek economies to maintain profit margins. As a result, lower priced homes have decreased in supply but higher priced homes have been less affected. Another resource movement stemming from high-land and high-building costs is the flow of funds into mobile homes. The sale of mobile homes, which was at about the 190,000 level in 1964, rose more than 450,000 in 1970. One mobile home is sold now for every three or four apartments or houses.

Under HUD's program of lower- and middle-income housing

---

[2] See *The New York Times,* Sunday, August 4, 1969, p. 47.

in the Housing Act of 1968, the number one goal was cost cutting. But the dominant view in the housing industry is that under optimal conditions, housing prices cannot be lowered immediately. Changes that can occur may be a slow disinflation or a change in the rate of increases in prices.

The high cost of residential housing is a function of anachronistic production methods. Single-unit houses constructed on a custom basis in city suburbs are built in almost exactly the same manner as houses built in the suburbs in 1910. Building materials have improved, but the basic construction methods for custom homes have changed little in the last 50 years. One construction expert noted, "If they placed the same emphasis on housing that they placed on landing men on the moon, then they'd get their housing. But, they aren't doing that."[3]

E. Financial Policy and Housing Supply

Restrictive monetary policies, which have slowed construction, have forced a variety of pressure to build up in housing markets.

Home buyers react to moderate downturns in mortgage rates and down payments by buying more readily. Housing demand usually rises while the rest of the economy experiences downturns. In an expanding economy, other industries bid for labor and other resources through higher prices and wages. With full employment the market for skilled craftsmen gets progressively tighter. The skilled craftsmen employed in large numbers in home construction are competed away. The most direct competition for residential housing resources is in industrial and commercial construction because the business community is anticipating high levels of business activity.

Credit competition increases occur as construction increases. Interest rates may rise because of the competition for available funds. Savers withdraw funds from their savings accounts to buy potential speculative securities. Bond yields, which usually climb more than mortgage rates, also tend to reduce the attractiveness of the mortgage lending. Banks and other credit sources find that the high industrial demand places pressures on the available

---

[3] Rex Selbe (a construction technology expert from the U. S. Gypsum Co.), *The Wall Street Journal*, Thursday, August 21, 1969, p. 24.

supply of funds, and low returns to banks from mortgage credit also discourage potential mortgage lending. Thus the market demand for funds for housing construction and the mobility of workers between the housing industry and other industries create a mutually competitive environment between the high growth in the economy as a whole and the growth in residential construction.

F. Demand and Supply of Housing—Summary

The housing available in the United States is a particular demand and supply problem. On the supply side, federal government programs to improve the quality of houses have produced a reduction in the housing stock available to low-income earners. On the demand side, distribution of income and residential construction costs have made it virtually impossible for most Americans to afford housing. A fundamental problem in housing for low-income families is that high costs make new housing beyond the reach of over half of the people in the United States. Since 70% of the families in the United States live on incomes of less than $10,000 a year, about two-thirds of all citizens are not able to buy new housing without some form of federal subsidy.

Furthermore, the housing inventory that is available exists in the form of old housing. About 90% of all housing that exists at any time is old housing. But the supply of old housing for low-income families has been decreasing because of federal programs. The highway programs of the federal government are displacing about 2500 households per year. The destruction of 96,400 housing units per year occurs in urban areas as a result of highway construction and urban renewal. This reduction in available housing is particularly significant for low-income individuals. About 35,100 owner-occupied households and 61,300 renter households will be displaced each year in urban areas because of these factors.

Future urban displacements will occur through urban and highway renewal. About 237,200 persons per year will be displaced by the programs. It is appropriate to assume that, at least, an equal number of these persons in surrounding areas are likely to be displaced or affected by this construction. For an eight-year period (from 1964 to 1972), it is estimated that a total of about 3.8 million persons may be forced to pay costs associated with housing displacements because of the urban highway, urban renewal, and highway construction, including about 1.9 million people who may be directly displaced. Although this total constitutes less than 2% of the entire population, it is significant.[4]

The housing supply situation for low-income householders in the United States has become worse in the past few years because of the slowdown in new housing starts. From 1962 to 1965 the average of 1.54 million units were started each year; but in 1966 only 1.25 million were started, and only 1.29 million were started in 1967. This 18% reduction in new housing starts occurred because of the high interest costs and lower demand for new housing. The demand for housing has been stimulated by high level prosperity, but the resulting combination of high demand and restriction of supply has created a tight housing market in metropolitan areas, that is, declining vacancies and upward pressure on rents.

I. GOVERNMENT AND HOUSING

Housing in America's urban centers is both a publicly and a privately offered good. The demand and supply forces for residential housing can be characterized as functioning to allocate resources into construction facilities for only selected consumers. The extent to which demand and supply forces in the private sector produce desirable qualities and quantities of residential housing is a determinant of the need for public entry into the field of housing.

A. Federal Action in Housing

The federal government has played an increasing role in the construction-industry market in the last few decades. The greatest government emphasis has been in residential construction. Generally stated, most government construction policies encourage home ownership.

Federal activity in the housing market began in the 1930s with the Home Loan Bank System and the National Housing Act of 1934. This NHA Act established a system of mortgage insurance

---

[4] *Economic Analysis and Efficiency in Government,* op. cit., pp. 307–308.

administered by the FHA and supplemented by the creation of the Federal Mortgage Association in 1938. Public housing, rent subsidies, and urban renewal were the principal focus of government activities in the 1940s and 1950s. Urban renewal was initiated in 1949 and broadened in 1954 to attempt to clear blighted areas, to provide locations for businesses, or to build moderate cost housing. By 1965 the Housing and Urban Development Act and the Department of Housing and Urban Development were created to coordinate many government programs in residential construction. Many other programs of the 1960s attempted to attack nonfiscal aspects of the delapidated inner core.

For example, the Model Cities Programs attempt to coordinate government policies in neighborhoods. The Model Cities Act, along with the Housing Act of 1968, provides subsidies to permit low-income families to purchase new homes, plus a new rental program for families. Both the Model Cities and Housing Act Programs rely almost exclusively on the effective role of private developers' and private mortgage financiers' reacting to subsidies payable directly to the mortgage lender.

The most significant element of the 1968 Housing Act is the recognition that urban housing problems exist. The act recognizes that the "Housing Problem" will not dissolve autonomously and that the free-enterprise market mechanism cannot or will not effectively solve the housing dilemmas in metropolitan areas. Existing federal housing policy now permits government action on a comprehensive basis. For example, the national government has enabling legislation which permits the bringing together of programs that focus on urban housing, income, and employment problems. The idea of coordinating inner-city problems is a prime objective in the Model Cities Act of 1966. This program explicitly recognizes that urban cores do not have the resources necessary to meet the critical problems they generate. The Model Cities Act does provide funds for the cities, identifies their needs, calculates costs, and embarks on solutions-oriented innovative programs. Unlike the Model Cities programs, money goes directly to cities of all sizes. The Model Cities' purpose is to permit cities to plan, develop, and carry out "local prepared comprehensive" city demonstration proposals, that is, (a) to rebuild or to revitalize slum or blighted areas, (b) to expand housing, jobs, and income opportunities, (c) to improve educational programs and facilities, (d) to combat disease and ill-health, (e) to reduce the incidence of crime and delinquency, (f) to enhance recreational and cultural opportunities, (g) to establish better access between homes and jobs, and (h) to improve living conditions for the people who reside in urban areas. Thus the federal government has a comprehensive program designed at the local level which concentrates funds for dealing simultaneously with the syndrome of problems in slum areas.

The Housing Act of 1968 has been labeled the Magna Carta to liberate our cities. The basic features of the act reaffirms the earlier housing-act goals of a "decent home and a suitable living environment for every American family." This act emphasizes programs to build both sales and rental housing for low-income families. This is a new important emphasis which was absent in earlier housing acts. The 1968 act calls for the development of programs to eliminate (within ten years) all substandard housing. Other goals of the act are to improve public housing, to provide additional assistance to large families, and to make easier the purchase of units of public housing by the occupants, to improve tenant services, to upgrade management personnel, to restrict the construction of high-rise apartment projects, and to encourage innovation in design.

Urban renewal projects were shifted from high-income luxury housing to low- and moderate-income housing. The act emphasizes improved programs for rehabilitation of housing through the monies available for relocation payments, housing codes administration, and enforcement activities. Another goal is to make money available to cooperative housing for housing services and to provide interest-rates subsidy programs. The act also sets up federal national mortgage association secondary market functions on a private basis and creates the unique services of the new Government Mortgage Association to provide funds for public housing.

The 1968 law is designed to provide mortgage insurance in high-risk areas plus government guarantees for the construction of "new town" developments. The "new towns" promote balance in low- and moderate-income housing. Other features of the act of 1968 include more funds for Model Cities programs, the provision of experimental housing programs to reduce costs, a National Homeowners Foundation to help the innovators of low- and moderate-income housing with money grants and loans, and a "National Housing Partnership with Private Industry" to attract more private sector resources into the low- and moderate-income housing construction.

In the 1968 act a potential was created whereby about one-half million low-income families would be able to buy new housing and another 700,000 units would provide for low- and moderate-income rentals. Subsidized interest rates for families meeting income qualifications and other subsidies could be made available for rental units for low-income families.

In previous legislation, Congress had been reluctant to provide funds for low-income housing programs and had minimized the impact of the housing program.

B. Public Housing Record

Although the public housing commitment of the federal government began soon after World War II, the pledges of the federal government have not been carried out. Only about 460,000 of the additional units in public housing have been completed in the 18 years of public-housing legislation from 1949 to 1967. The total of all public housing was only 633,000 units. In the earlier years of public housing, the programs were not essentially devoted to urban or low-income problems. Urban needs and urban programs and low-income family needs have only recently become primary concerns of both public and private participants in public-housing policy.

Public-housing emphasis in the United States is usually misunderstood. The focus of the federal public-housing activity has been on providing adequate numbers and quality of residences for middle-income people, not low-income families. For example,

. . . yet the reality of public housing in New York City is that, historically and up to the present time, it has provided a major source of housing for the working class. It has been able to do this by rigorously avoiding making public housing a form of welfare housing. Historically, New York's public housing has been built for a relatively stable, substantially employed, sector of the city's population. As a result there has been considerable stability of the residents.[5]

---

[5] George Sternlieb, "New York Housing—A Study in Immobilism," *The Public Interest,* No. 16, Summer 1969, p. 133.

The public-housing programs have been recently more oriented to needs of the urban inner-city dweller and other urban poor. On a historical basis the federal public-housing-efforts have had little positive impact on the quality of life of the poor urban families who have most needed better housing. The public-housing program at the end of the 1960 decade was experiencing financial deficits and program erosion. For example, in St. Louis about 50% of all apartments in public-housing projects are vacant because of undesirable living conditions and rampant crime. In other metropolitan areas the public-housing authorities have conceded the existence of heating, maintenance, and repair problems because projects cannot support maintenance from their own expenses. Rents have been increased and operating costs have been larger than federal subsidy. In the summer of 1969, George Romney[6] noted that the country's major housing authorities were near bankruptcy.

The cities involved were New York, Chicago, Los Angeles, Philadelphia, Detroit, Washington, St. Louis, San Francisco, Boston, Kansas City, Columbus (Ohio), New Haven, Newark, Omaha, and Louisville. If this pattern of financial stringency continues, 200 more local authorities soon will be in financial trouble. The basic source of the problem is that federal subsidies do not cover the inflationary high operating expenses. These costs must be paid by rents. To keep rents relatively low, HUD makes yearly grants to the local authorities to cover interest payments and debt services on construction bonds. But the construction of the housing must be financed by bonds sold through local and semiindependent authorities. Both of these financial features tend to preclude expansion and improvement in public housing.

The reasons for failure of federal public-housing programs are many. For example, local housing officials have often argued that Congress fixed ceilings that were too low on the number of housing units, and these authorized units in public-housing account for the slow pace of construction. Congress has, in fact, set authorization limits below those originally expected to have been established in the 1949 act. Although the ceilings have changed

---

[6] George Romney, Secretary of Housing and Urban Development, *The New York Times*, October 12, 1969, p. 1.

from year to year, they have typically averaged about 35,000 units of public housing. By late 1965 the yearly ceiling was set at 60,000 units, but cities have never built housing at the rate or the level authorized by Congress. Perhaps New York City is the exception, since it has moved ahead and has approximately 150,000 public housing units in operation. But for the country as a whole the public housing starts have been below the ceilings every year.

The National Commission on Urban Problems indicates that the public-housing program has been slowed to a faltering walk largely by economic class and racial antagonisms. Other factors have also played a role, but nonclass racial issues are secondary. The Commission expressed the view that it may be futile either to pretend that some new gimmick in the subsidy or other formula would make much difference in hitting at the basic problems of public housing.

C. Income-Tax-Sourced Housing Subsidies

The federal government has, through the Internal Revenue Service, administered a perverse income subsidy for United States homeowners. The present federal income tax code contains a particular pattern of distribution of income that is of significant importance to the demand and supply of housing. As a result of the administration of the internal revenue code, there is a subsidy for certain housing for individuals in selected income classes.[7]

Analysis indicates that a large tax subsidy accrues to homeowners because they pay no tax on imputed rent and are allowed to deduct interest paid on mortgages as well as local government property taxes. Other smaller benefits accrue to rental housing owners through accelerated depreciation rates. Since subsidies of all types from taxes will influence allocation of resources as well as income distribution, these tax subsidies affect the consumption of housing and influence the determination of housing stocks. The impact on income distribution stems from the large benefits that accrue to upper-income homeowners. The tax subsidy is equivalent to a direct housing subsidy but only for selected groups. The administration of the tax code discriminates

---

[7] Henry Aaron, "Income Taxes and Housing," *The American Economic Review,* December 1970, Vol. LXV, pp. 789–806.

against the lower-income people or individuals with asset holdings.

. . . tax benefits provide largest benefits to the recipients of larger than average income as experienced with wealth, is typically not limited to their own homes. They provide negligible aid to low income households, most of whom have not been vouchsafed the salutory discipline of property management.[8]

. . . By increasing demand for housing services, a highly capital intensive commodity, tax benefits probably raise yields on capital in general. This increase affects all recipients of income from capital.

Furthermore, it raises the price of capital intensive commodities such as housing, relative to the price of other commodities. Since tax benefits on rental properties are so much smaller than those available to homeowners, the former may do little more than offset the price increasing effects, through capital costs, of the latter.[9]

Aaron characterizes the benefits that accrue from the particular tax code in a fact as "capricious and without rationale."

The federal personal income tax subsidy for housing is the government's largest direct form of subsidy for housing. Its effect is to give greater subsidy to people who need it least. The wealthiest one-fifth of the population in our country receive twice as much of that income tax housing subsidy as do the poorest fifth. This indirect housing subsidy will not aid in the building of needed housing in the United States.

D. Housing Policy Assessment

Housing production has decreased while housing costs have increased. Federal efforts to increase production and to hold down costs have not been effective. Only modest changes have occurred in housebuilding methods. Future improvements and productivity must overcome resistance from materials producers, craft unions, local building codes, and officials who have vested interests in existing housing programs. Federal government financial support, which has not been adequate in the past, will be necessary to improve construction methods. During the

---

[8] Ibid., p. 803.
[9] Ibid.

1960s the federal government policy on housing encouraged non-profit groups to undertake housing for moderate- and low-income citizens. These efforts were well intended, but financial resources were limited and housing gains from these groups were modest. The federal policies from the Housing Act of 1968 have had only slight influence in slowing the flow of mortgage funds and property insurance coverage from inner city neighborhoods. Public activity in the last decade has been characterized by planning for the potential development of housing services such as sewage and water and mass transportation. The federal government has moved to encourage comprehensive planning and to strengthen local public authorities in metropolitan areas, but without significant improvement in the fragmentation of governmental urban responsibility.

The Model Cities program is significant legislation because it reflects a comprehensive approach to the syndrome of urban problems. The Model Cities Act was designed to improve the coordination of all the services that affect disadvantaged people in deteriorating neighborhoods. Under Model Cities the control of the implementation is basically in the hands of local mayors. It is apparent because of the constraint on money plus the malaise in local administrations that the response by mayors is not characterized by vigor and innovation. The money constraint on the program limits Model Cities' effectiveness. Other programs like revenue sharing must provide additional funds for the Model Cities' coordination of programs such as job training and education to be implemented.

. . . there are good reasons to wonder about the depth of the national commitment to housing in urban improvement. Time and again, what the Congress has given, the Congress has all but taken away by cutting appropriations for programs such as rent supplements, Model Cities, and the administration of the fair housing law. . . .

We are not likely to see in the next several years a burst of legislation in housing and urban development comparable to that which occurred in the '60's, particularly during the latter part of the decade. This need not mean a slowing in the performance level; it could mean the start of volume production from social inventions and institutional machinery put into place since 1961. Congress has set high goals for housing, and many new tools are at hand. It is time for absorption and integration of these new programs. Application of good management skills and a streamlining of administrative procedures could help close the gap between promise and fulfillment.[10]

E. Policy Choices

Solutions-oriented housing policies are probably in the counter intuitive category and may run counter to the direct solution of simply providing improved housing for the individual poor urban family.

But policies that permit all low-income families to become effective participants in the housing market are essential in the long term.

Future policy should be directed to change the status of housing for the poor, by focusing on the basic supply and demand forces for housing. Policies that shift either the demand or the supply curve in the market for housing must affect the price in the total housing market.

Policies that may influence supply include long-term loans at below market interest rates. The high interest charges, plus the high cost of existing homes, militates against the poor in buying new housing. Credit policies or high down payments and high interest rates reduce the effective demand of the poor for new or high-quality housing.

A different group of policies could be implemented to increase effective demand. Federal programs that provide subsidies as rental allowances plus direct income for the poor are the best approaches.[11]

Housing improvement programs can be designed directly to redistribute the income to urban poor, or indirectly by programs to train the urban poor in improved skills or by reducing racial tensions and raising morale and civic commitment of the urban poor.

The redistribution of income to the poor has demand side

---

[10] Morton J. Schussheim, "Toward a New Housing Policy," *Committee for Economic Development,* Supplementary Paper No. 2, New York, 1969, pp. 61–62.

[11] John B. Lansing, C. W. Clifton, and J. N. Morgan, *New Homes for Poor People* (Institute for Social Research, University of Michigan, Ann Arbor, 1969), p. 68.

effects as would training or upgrading skills. The efforts to reduce racial tensions, which include eliminating the material bases
for grievances, may also be made at the same time that the distribution of income to the poor is improved. The local control
of community institutions and promotion of home ownerships by
the poor, plus the dispersal of ghetto populations into other
neighborhoods, have the effect not only of improving the housing environment but also of raising the civic commitment to better
housing on the part of the urban poor. Thus each housing program has alternatives that are not directly related to improving
housing, but would have direct impact on the capacity of the
urban poor to participate more effectively in the existing housing
market. The nonhousing alternatives of housing programs include
increased employment opportunities, which involves moving industry into the ghetto, improved transportation systems, improved public services in the ghetto, improved inner city schools,
on the job training, vocational and skills training schools in the
inner city, and the development of the political power of individuals residing in the inner city.

No isolated or simplistic policies can solve the urban housing
problem, nor can improve housing for the poor.

Policy makers must avoid the implementation of counter productive policies, whether directed at housing or designed to influence housing accidentally. It is quite clear, for example, that
urban renewal policies have adversely affected the supply of low-
rent housing. Current property tax administration has produced
adverse effects on the central-city housing supply. Discrimination
and zoning restrictions as well as building codes have slowed the
expansion of housing options for urban residents. In Dick Netzer's
terms, "A wide range of policies, new and traditional, each of
them having a modest impact on the underlying problems, seems
necessary if there is to be massive overall impact."[12]

Improved housing for the urban poor is not likely to result
from housing, public or private, which is specifically designed
for the poor. In the past, the urban poor have upgraded their
housing by "moving up to" housing formerly occupied by higher

---

[12] Dick Netzer, *Economics in Urban Problems* (New York: Basic Books,
1970), p. 107.

income groups. "In effect the housing improvement for the poor comes through a 'filtering down process' that results from the aging or other economic and social factors that account for the middle income families moving from one house to another."[13] Therefore, public policies that bring about increases in the rate of new housing starts or that increase the pace of turnover of housing for middle-income families tends to improve housing standards for both the high- and low-income groups.

F. Quality of Housing

In the analysis of factors accounting for the quality of housing in central cities, it appears that differences in the proportion of substandard dwellings within and among different cities at any given time and through overtime may be explained by the relative demand for poor versus good quality housing.[14]

By far the most important determinant of the condition of dwelling units is the income level of their inhabitants. Not only is the association between condition and income quite close, but the quantitative response of conditions to income changes is very strong indeed . . . .

On the whole there seems to be little evidence that variations in the relative quantities of poor- and good-quality housing are importantly affected by differences in their relative supply . . ., the positive association between poor dwelling-unit condition and crowding is largely due to the fact that they are closely related aspects of low income demand for housing.[15]

The income position of potential homeowners and conditions in the money markets play a significant role in the pattern of demand for new housing. The ability of potential homeowners to actively compete for available mortgage money is a determinant in the total demand for homes. Income levels and access to funds in effect determine who in our system can buy housing. The income constraint, if added to discrimination, is particularly apparent in the pattern of housing that is purchased by low-income minorities in urban areas.

---

[13] Wilbur R. Thompson, *A Preface to Urban Economics* (Baltimore: Johns Hopkins Press, Published for Resources for the Future, Inc., 1968), p. 296.
[14] Muth, *Cities and Housing,* op. cit., p. 325.
[15] Ibid., p. 326.

II. SUBSTANDARD HOUSING—A CENTRAL CITY PROBLEM

The substandard housing in the United States is a small proportion of the total national housing stock. Substandard housing stock is relatively higher in small towns or rural areas than in large cities. More than 45% of the total dilapidated stock of housing is located in rural areas and accounts for about one-fourth of the occupied rural housing units. Only about 7% of occupied units in central cities report plumbing deficiencies, and this number is believed to have diminished during the last five years.[16]

The poor housing component of the contemporary urban crisis syndrome is not a separate problem but is inexorably entwined with other problems. Poor and bad housing does not generate slums. Poor housing is symptomatic of income distribution and racial discrimination problems.

Substandard housing usually occurs in urban centers and segregrated areas and among minority low-income groups concentrated in the central cities. The United States Commission on Urban Problems observed that the percentage of the poor living in substandard housing did not seem to be particularly high, but of particular concern to the commission was the relationship of poor housing and poverty level incomes—particularly renters' income.

Clearly, if many poor households escape rock bottom bad housing, there is little comfort to be drawn from these facts, indicating as they do that such escape can only mean truly curtailed expenditures for other basic necessities such as food, clothing, or medical care.[17]

The relationship of poverty and bad housing is illustrated in central cities. One-third of the housing units found in poverty areas are on less than one-quarter of the land area. Low-income

---

[16] See data for 1960 and 1966, HUD Program Memorandum, FY 1968, FY 1972; Data for 1940 and 1950, *Statistical Abstract of the United States,* 1967 U. S. Bureau of the Census; Population of the U. S. by Metropolitan and non-Metropolitan Residents, April 1960 and 1966, Series P20, No. 163, 1967.

[17] *Report of the National Commission on Urban Problems,* Part II, "Housing Programs," Chapter I, p. 33.

or poverty districts in metropolitan areas contain 80% of all housing units occupied by nonwhites in central cities; they contain 75% of the substandard units in central cities, nine out of ten of the substandard units occupied by nonwhites in central cities, over 50% of the overcrowded units in these central cities, five out of six of the overcrowded units occupied by nonwhites in these central cities, 40% of all housing structures built before 1940 in these central cities, of which about 33% are 100 years older, and five out of six of all structures build before 1940 that are lived in by nonwhites in these central cities.[18]

Housing in cities, thus, is differentiated in spatial distribution by ethnic groups, costs, as well as economic class or race.

Harlem still presents a very substantial refuge for many of the poor blacks. But Harlem is a tired, middle-aged community now, with incomes much higher and the proportion of children much lower than in "growth areas" for the poor. The largest of these is the Bedford-Stuyvesant area of Brooklyn. Sections of the Bronx too serve as refuge for the poor. Indeed, the South Bronx is rapidly becoming an environment whose impact on its inhabitants may be even more deleterious than that of the older slums. The lower east side, with its wall to wall, five and six story walkup old-law tenements, has partaken of every population shift in the cities history. The current surge is the replacement of Jews by substantially Puerto Rican and Negro population. But the lower east side is, like Harlem, an area moving gradually into decay. Like Harlem, it is steadily losing population.[19]

In the ghetto the relationship of employment, housing, transportation, and income is determined by low performance or low quality standards of institutions and economic activity. This is also the significant relationship that exists for any sector of any urban area. These economic interrelationships vary in status but do exist in all metropolitan areas. The fundamental economic relationships will prescribe the differentials in the qualities of life in urban areas. The interrelationships may or may not produce distortions in overall metropolitan development. In other

---

[18] Ibid., p. 36.
[19] George Sternlieb, "New York's Housing: A Study in Immobilism," *The Public Interest*, No. 16, Summer 1969, p. 126.

words, the effective demand for land use and economic activity in the inner city and in the suburb are determined by economic factors. If residents in the inner city have low incomes and are confronted with few high-income job opportunities because of difficulties in travel to job location, or inadequate training and skills to enter higher paying employment, the economic vitality of the city will reflect the pattern of demand for goods and services related to low levels of income. The low income and declining effective demand for goods and services with the inner city is the significant variable in the relationship. Because of a variety of factors, including poor education and economic and legal discrimination, many central city residents with low incomes happen to be blacks. The quality of their life is a function of their effective income level or economic demand. The existence of residents of minority groups in inner cities has not caused deteriorated or delapidated housing. The interrelationships of variables which have forced the minority groups to exert effective demand for the low quality of housing and other goods and services is the appropriate focus.[20]

---

[20] Banfield argues that housing differentials for the Negro are related not to race but to other characteristics, perhaps class. In that argument he indicates that Negroes spend as much as a third more for housing than whites do at any given income level and that it is not clear that segregation in housing leads to higher prices for equivalent quality for Negroes. Banfield cites studies made in Chicago that indicate that when differences in location, occupation, income and other variables are taken into account, the Negroes' costs of housing are not very different from those of whites. In Chicago, at least, the Negro pays about the same rent and lives at about the same density as the white. . . . "Much of what appears (especially to Negroes) as race prejudice is really class prejudice, or at any rate, class antipathy. Similarly, much of what appears (especially to whites) as 'Negro' behavior is really lower-class behavior. The lower class is relatively large non-negro; it appears even larger than it is to those whites who fail to distinguish a Negro who exhibits outward signs—lack of skill, low income, slum housing, and etc.,—which in a white would mark him as lower class, from one whose culture is working, middle or even upper class, but whose opportunities has been limited by discrimination and whose income is low." Edward C. Banfield, *The Unheavenly City* (Boston: Little, Brown & Co., 1970), pp. 71 and 76.

9

The Economics of the Ghetto

Most large cities in the United States exhibit a phenomenon that is loosely described as a "ghetto." The term "ghetto" is a difficult one to conceptualize, and means widely different things among various users. For example, Kenneth Clark, a noted Negro psychologist, describes or identifies the ghetto by the sociopsychological conditions existent within these regions.[1] Others have chosen the alternative of simply describing the ghetto along racial lines, identifying it as a racial enclave. This process, however, does not account for the fact that many of those living in poverty and in inner-city areas are not members of ethnic minorities. A third alternative is to delineate the ghetto by economic criteria. In this case the ghetto would be characterized as an area exhibiting low incomes, low productivity, inadequate and inferior education, health and sanitary facilities, substandard housing, and the like. The difficulty with using economic criteria to designate the ghetto is that it fails to distinguish adequately between what is a ghetto and what is simply a slum area. Conceptually, at least, these terms should be distinguishable. A fourth alternative is to identify the ghetto in terms of a region characterized by limited freedom—freedom in terms of the alternative choices and opportunities available to residents—alternatives, choices, and opportunities in jobs, housing, education and health care, and social interaction.

---

[1] Kenneth Clark, *The Dark Ghetto* (New York: Harper & Row, 1965).

162

The use of the first two designations, the social-psychological and the racial enclave criteria, does not seem particularly productive. These fail to distinguish between a ghetto in the inner city and a high-income, predominantly Caucasion, suburban enclave. The fourth alternative, describing the ghetto in terms of the range of choices available to its residents appears to be the better definition. The limitation of the range of choice of the ghetto residents is, in many cases, a function of his economic condition, although in many others it is related to racial discrimination.

A. The Genesis and Perpetuation of a Ghetto

The attempt to determine what causes and perpetuates a ghetto leads to a pattern of mutual causality and interactions. This process of interacting causality has been called "cumulative circular causation."[2] The process becomes even more complex when an effort is made to extract the economic causes from the social, political, and psychological ones. However, in approaching the subject of ghettos of urban regions it becomes important to have an economic frame of reference. Figure 9-1 indicates many of the factors that interact in this process of "cumulative circular causation."

1. The overwhelming reality for the nonwhite is racial discrimination—social, political, and economic. Racial discrimination results in economic discrimination in two ways. First it tends to exclude the Negro from access to jobs and other sources of income. Second, the market mechanism is designed to discriminate through its rationing function against those who have purchasing power inferior to that of other consumers in the market. In many cases Negroes, because of low incomes, are simply priced out of the market and unable to purchase commodities (because of their cost) that would make for a decent standard of living. Racial discrimination and racially influenced economic discrimination lead to segregation, and an informal although not inflexible, apartheid situation in metropolitan areas.

2. Segregation and the economic circumstances of the ghetto

---

[2] Gunnar Myrdal, *An American Dilemma* (New York: McGraw-Hill, 1964), pp. 75–78.

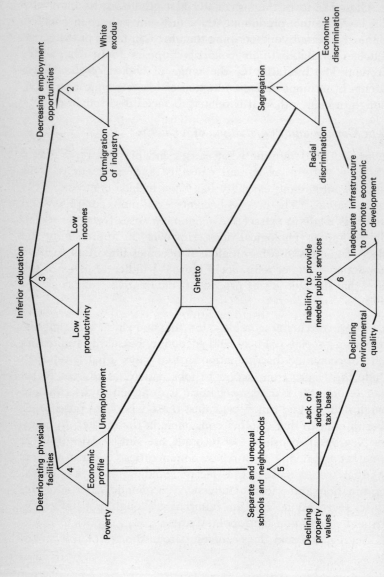

Figure 9-1

create an environment that is not conducive to the retention of industry and white population located in central-city areas. The locational influences that originally attracted and held industry in the central city are gradually eroded. Positive locational factors such as rapidity of contact and communication and proximity of the urban market are being offset rapidly by technological improvements in both communications and transportation. Technology is offsetting the remaining positive locational factor of the ghetto—a cheap unskilled supply of labor. Industrial operations are becoming increasingly capital-intensive, requiring less labor, and higher skills levels of those workers who remain employed. These factors have resulted in a trend of industry moving out of the central-city areas and into the suburban rings.

The phenomena of increasing racial concentration, deteriorating physical environments, and the outward movement of industry have created a climate that encourages those with the social and economic freedom to do so to leave the ghetto area. The result has been the massive exodus of whites from central-city areas to the suburbs, causing the ghettos to become increasingly nonwhite and poor.

Both of these factors, the out-migration of industry and the white exodus, have caused a diminuation in the employment opportunities available to ghetto residents. Employment opportunities increasingly are located in the suburban rings, and even menial service occupations in the white community are in the suburbs. Thus a nonwhite desiring employment must travel long distances from the central-city area to the suburbs to find and hold jobs. The availability and quality of public transportation facilities then becomes of primary importance in determining the ability of ghetto residents to reach existing opportunities.

3. A phenomenon exists in the ghetto that is described as "the vicious circle of poverty." Decreasing employment opportunities are in part responsible for the low incomes of ghetto residents. Low income results in the inability to obtain adequate education and skills level and, in some cases, to require a proper nutritional level in their diets.[3] Malnutrition, inferior education

---

[3] Evidence is now available that protein deficiencies in diets can cause mental retardation in a child and that protein deficiency in a mother during pregnancy also can result in the mental retardation of her child.

and skills level causes low productivity in the labor factor in the ghetto. Low productivity results in low incomes and the chain of causation begins again.

4. Conditions 2 and 3 result in the economic profile of ghetto residents. Because of the combination of decreasing employment opportunities, inferior education, and low productivity, extensive unemployment exists within the ghetto. Thus the ghetto residents live in poverty, sometimes abject poverty, in the midst of a rapidly deteriorating physical environment. The physical facilities of these areas had been initially constructed by white residents and then abandoned as they aged, and the quality of the environment deteriorates with the present residents because they are unable to maintain these facilities as a result of their age, rate of deterioration, and the residents' low income.

5. The cumulative interaction of these factors then leads to the classic image of the ghetto, the separate and segregated environment possessing schools and other public facilities inferior to the ones that exist in other areas of the metropolis. The rapid deterioration of the physical environment results in declining property values. This combined with the low incomes of the region and the out-migration of industry results in the lack of an adequate tax base to provide the needed public services for the area.

6. The lact of an adequate tax base to support the necessary public services in the ghetto region results in a situation in which the services must be subsidized by other regions of the metropolitan area if they are to be supplied. The ghetto area is characterized by inferior public facilities such as roads, education, public health, sanitation, and education—public services that are necessary to create a level of environmental quality in which the individual does not suffer from the dehabilitating affects of his environment.

The inability to provide needed public services also results in the inefficiency of the services that are termed "infrastructure" or "social overhead capital." These are usually publicly provided services, for instance, the techniques of rapid communication, energy sources such as electricity and gas, and roads and other transportation facilities that provide the base necessary for economic development to occur. These facilities are available for use by industrial firms and their supporting service industries and the labor forces employed by these firms. It has been charged by black militants that ghetto areas have been systematically discriminated against in the supply of intrastructure facilities, condemning these areas to a perpetual state of underdevelopment by depriving them of the basis on which economic growth can occur.

The sum of deteriorating fiscal facilities in the ghetto, inferior education, low incomes, separate and unequal schools in neighborhoods, and the inability to provide needed public services and infrastructure result in a rapidly declining level of environmental quality in the ghetto region. The low level of environmental quality militates against the possibility of an individual breaking out of this chain of interacting circular causation. The whole environment of the ghetto interacts in a way that tends to lock a ghetto resident into the region and to deprive him of opportunities for material betterment that are available to residents of other regions of urban areas.

Available data support the contention that the ghetto exhibits these characteristics of economic underdevelopment. For a study of urban economics it is relevant to investigate, in particular, data on population, poverty, housing, and employment.

I POPULATION SHIFTS AND GHETTO CONCENTRATION

It is projected that the population of the United States will increase by 41% between 1960 to 1985. The percentage increase for whites will be 37.1%; that for the nonwhite population, of which 92% is Negro, will be 68.2%, or a 31.1% greater increase in the nonwhite population. If these projections are realized, approximately 14% of the population of the United States will be nonwhite.[4]

The National Commission of Urban Problems has suggested that the United States is facing a population "implosion."[5] This

---

[4] *Report of the National Commission on Urban Problems,* Part I, "Population, Poverty and Race," pp. 4–5.

[5] Ibid., p. 7.

rapid population increase, to a large extent, will be contained within given geographical regions—the urban areas of this country. "The central cities, which already contain half of the nation's non-white population, will concentrate an even greater share of the non-white residents in the future if the trends of the last few decades are maintained.[6] Reference to Table 9-1 indicates

Table 9-1. Color Composition of Metropolitan Areas,[a] Central Cities, and SMSA Rings, 1960 and Projected 1985

Residence and Color	United States		
	1985	1960	Change
SMSA	100.0	100.0	
White	84.9	88.3	− 3.4
Nonwhite	15.1	11.7	+ 3.4
Central city	100.0	100.0	
White	69.3	82.2	−12.9
Nonwhite	30.7	17.8	+12.9
SMSA Ring	100.0	100.0	
White	93.9	94.8	− 0.9
Nonwhite	6.1	5.2	+ 0.9

Source. United States Bureau of the Census, *United States Census of Population, 1960, Selected Area Reports, Type of Place,* Final Report PC (3)-1E, Table 1; and Appendix A, Table A-2.
[a] 1960 boundaries of SMSA's used for 1960; 1967 boundaries used for 1985.

that the nonwhite population of metropolitan areas of 50,000 or more will increase by 3.4% with a corresponding increase in the white population. The central city is decreasing in terms of white population and is projected to increase its nonwhite population by approximately 12.9% by 1985. If these trends continue, by 1985 more than three-fourths of the nation's Negroes will live in metropolitan areas, and 85% of them will live in central cities.[7] The central-city areas of the United States are becoming increasingly nonwhite and increasingly concentrated. However it should be noted that if present trends continue, the population of central-city areas will increase by 13% and that of suburban

---

[6] Ibid., p. 11.
[7] Ibid., p. 13.

areas or rings will grow by 106%. Thus, although the population of central cities will increase, it will become a smaller percentage of total urban population.[8]

II. INCOME AND POVERTY OF GHETTO RESIDENTS

The percentage of the nonwhite population of the United States living in poverty is much greater than the percentage of the white population that falls into this category of economic deprivation, although significant improvement was recorded for both groups in the decade of the 1960s. In 1960 approximately 55% of the nonwhite population was categorized as living below the poverty line, as compared to 18% of the white population. The situation had improved by 1967 to the extent that the incidence of poverty of nonwhites was 35% and that of whites was 10%. Data indicate (Table 9-2) that the economic conditions of the Negro relative to the white has been improving during this period. The median Negro family income increased from 55% of white family median income in 1962 to 62% by 1967. In addition, the percentage increase in black incomes in the latter part of the 1960s was consistently greater than the percentage increase in white incomes.

Superficial inspection of this information might lead to the assumption that the position of the Negro has improved when compared to that of the white. However, this data should be treated cautiously. To a significant degree this change can be attributed to black migration from the low-wage areas of the South and from rural to urban areas.[9] In addition, the absolute difference between the median incomes of whites and the median incomes of Negros has increased throughout this period (Table 9-2, Column 2). This means that the economic disparity between the circumstances of the Negro and that of the white has been increasing rather than decreasing. If the hypothesis is correct that the origins of the urban riots are based in the deprivation of Negros relative to whites (relative-deprivation hy-

---

[8] Ibid.,p. 9.
[9] See J. Gwartney, "Changes in the Non-white/White Income Ratio, 1939–67," *American Economic Review,* Vol. LX (December 1970), p. 872.

Table 9-2

	Index of Negro and Other Nonwhite Races' General Improvement	Position of Negroes and Other Nonwhite Races Relative to Whites in the Economy
	Negro and Other Nonwhite Percent of White Median Family Income	Difference Between Median Family Incomes of Whites and Negroes and Other Nonwhites (White Median Family Income—Nonwhite Median Family Income)
1947	51.1	$1543
1950	54.3	1576
1952	56.8	1776
1954	55.5	1929
1956	52.6	2365
1958	51.2	2589
1960	55.4	2602
1961	53.4	2790
1962	53.4	2907
1963	52.9	3083
1964	56.0	3019
1965	55.0	3257
1966	58.0	3118
1967	62.1	3133
1968	63.0	3347

Source. United States Bureau of the Census, Current Population Reports, Series P-60 No. 66, "Income in 1968 of Families and Persons in the United States," United States Government Printing Office, Washington, D. C., 1969.

pothesis), the increasing economic disparities between the two races will lead to greater frustration and the possibility of greater and, perhaps, castastrophic urban disorders.

The distribution of the poor within the city and in rural areas is significant in terms of assessing the possibilities for the city and the alternatives for ghetto areas. Table 9-3 indicates that metropolitan areas contain approximately 65% of the population of the United States and more than one-half of the nation's poor. However, the concentration of nonwhites in cities and the concentration on nonwhite poor in these areas is greater than the average for the nation as a whole. Approximately 68% of the nonwhite residents in the United States are concentrated

Table 9-3. Distribution of Total Population, Contrasted with Distribution of Total Poor, Population, by Type of Place, 1966

	All Persons		White Persons		Nonwhite Persons	
	Percent of Total United States Population	Percent of United States Poor	Percent of Total United States Population	Percent of United States Poor	Percent of Total United States Population	Percent of United States Poor
Metropolitan	64.7%	51.0%	64.3%	50.0%	67.9%	53.0%
Central City	30.2	31.5	27.0	26.5	53.4	43.6
Ring	34.6	19.5	37.3	23.5	14.5	9.6
Nonmetropolitan	35.3	49.0	37.5	50.0	32.1	46.8
	100.0	100.0	100.0	100.0	100.0	100.0

Source. "Counting the Poor: Before and After Federal Income-Support Programs," (Population estimates derived from special tabulations made by the Bureau of the Census from the Current Population Survey for March 1967).

in cities and 53%, or over one-half, the nonwhite poor are located in metropolitan areas. A majority of the nonwhites in these metropolitan areas are concentrated within the central city, although approximately 56% of the nonwhite poor live outside of the central city either in the metropolitan ring or in nonmetropolitan areas. Thus the picture emerges of the central cities increasing rapidly in population density, and increasingly concentrating the poor within these regions.

III. CENTRAL-CITY HOUSING AND HOUSING DENSITY

Housing discrimination and job discrimination are two leading causal factors creating barriers to outmigration of nonwhites from central-city areas. Discrimination in housing has resulted in housing segregation and has created living conditions within the ghetto area that are a national shame. Statistics are readily available to document the magnitude of this catastrophe. Data indicate that 23.3% of the land area of central cities in 1960 were designated as poverty areas and that these poverty areas of central cities contain:[10]

1. 33% of all the cities' housing units.
2. 76% of the substandard housing units.
3. 54% of the overcrowded units.
4. 45% of the vacant housing units.
5. 41% of the units and structures over 20 years old.
6. 42% of the units in multiunit structures.
7. 44% of the renter-occupied units, but only 19% of all the owner-occupied units in the central cities.

The housing density in central-city poverty areas is also much greater than that of other regions of the cities. There were approximately 83,071 housing units per square miles within the ghetto areas, which was roughly 64% more than in the other areas of these same cities. It should be noticed, however, that more central-city poverty area housing units were vacant, so

---

[10] National Commission on Urban Problems, "Housing Conditions in Urban Poverty Areas," *Research Report Number 9* (Washington, D.C. United States Government Printing Office, 1968), p. 7.

that if the comparison is made in terms of occupied housing units the density figure is reduced to 59% higher in central-city poverty areas than elsewhere in these metropolitan regions.[11]

Housing, perhaps, represents one of the greatest failures of federal policy in recent history. In the 1969 Economic Report, the President states that:

The area of housing is the most outstanding example of the Federal Government's failure to fulfill its commitment. It is now two decades since the passage of the Housing Act of 1949. We have not yet constructed the number of housing units contemplated for the first six years of that act. According to the report of the National Commission on Urban Problems, we have demolished more housing by public action—under such programs as highways and urban renewals —than has been built under all federally aided programs. There are approximately 11 million sub-standard and over-crowded housing units. Yet, new housing starts total less than 1.5 million units per year, far below the number required to effect a rapid replacement of substandard units and to provide for an expanding population.[12]

IV. INCIDENCE OF UNEMPLOYMENT IN GHETTO REGIONS

Exclusion from other than menial job opportunities because of lack of education or skills attainment or because of racial discrimination has caused the unemployment rate of nonwhites to be approximately double that of whites during the last two decades (Table 9-4). The high unemployment rate and the high incidence of poverty among nonwhite are causally related. A study of the 20 largest metropolitan areas of the United States in 1967 indicated that the unemployment rate was much higher in central cities than in suburban areas, as might be expected in view of the high concentration of nonwhites in central cities (Table 9-5). However the unemployment rate for nonwhites was high and approximately equal in both the central

---

11 Ibid.

12 *The 1969 Economic Report,* Report of the Joint Economic Committee, Congress of the United States, in the January 1969 Economic Report of the President, April 1, 1969 (Washington, D.C., United States Government Printing Office), p. 47.

Table 9-4. Unemployment Rates,ᵃ 1948 to 1967, and 1968 (First Six Months)

	Nonwhite	White	Ratio: Nonwhite to White
1948	5.2	3.2	1.6
1949	8.9	5.6	1.6
1950	9.0	4.9	1.8
1951	5.3	3.1	1.7
1952	5.4	2.8	1.9
1953	4.5	2.7	1.7
1954	9.9	5.0	2.0
1955	8.7	3.9	2.2
1956	8.3	3.6	2.3
1957	7.9	3.8	2.1
1958	12.6	6.1	2.1
1959	10.7	4.8	2.2
1960	10.2	4.9	2.1
1961	12.4	6.0	2.1
1962	10.9	4.9	2.2
1963	10.8	5.0	2.2
1964	9.6	4.6	2.1
1965	8.1	4.1	2.0
1966	7.3	3.3	2.2
1967	7.4	3.4	2.2
1968 (first 6 months seasonally adjusted)	6.8	3.2	2.1

Source. United States Department of Labor, Bureau of Labor Statistics, as published in *Recent Trends in Social and Economic Conditions of Negroes in the United States,* July 1968.

ᵃ The unemployment rate is the percent unemployed in the civilian labor force.

city and the suburban area, indicating that it was difficult for nonwhites to obtain a job in either area.[13]

The Report of the National Advisory Commission on Civil Disorders indicates that a major causal factor in the urban riots was underemployment, persons "holding menial jobs that re-

[13] *Report of the National Commission on Urban Problems,* Part I, "Population, Poverty and Race," op. cit., p. 26.

Table 9-5. Unemployment in Central Cities and Suburbs of the Twenty Largest Metropolitan Areas,[a] 1967

	Unemployment Rate			Number Unemployed (in Thousands)	
	Nonwhite	White	Ratio: Nonwhite to White	Nonwhite	White
Central cities	7.6	3.7	2.1	222	332
Adult men	4.9	2.8	1.8	75	148
Adult women	6.6	3.5	1.8	76	109
Teenagers	31.6	11.5	2.4	71	73
Suburbs	7.0	3.1	2.3	53	107

Source. United States Department of Labor, Bureau of Labor Statistics.

[a] In the 20 largest metropolitan areas in 1960.

quired less than the skills levels which they had attained." Although no data is available on underemployment, the U. S. Department of Labor, in 1968, began to publish a new national subemployment measure.[14] Table 9-6 presents data on the subemployment rate in major ghetto areas in 1966. It indicates that the unemployment figures greatly understate the impact of racial discrimination on employment patterns, with the subemployment figures of much greater magnitude than corresponding unemployment figures.

In 1965 two efforts were made to calculate the economic costs of discrimination. The first of them indicated that the income differential between a Negro and a white undertaking the same job with the same educational attainment would be approximately $1000.[15]

---

[14] *Recent Trends in Social and Economic Conditions of Negroes in the United States,* United States Department of Labor, Bureau of Labor Statistics, Washington, D.C., United States Government Printing Office, July 1968, p. 17. This includes: (1) number of workers unemployed fifteen weeks or more, and (2) workers who made less than $3000 in 1966 for year-round, full-time work.

[15] Paul N. Siegel, "On the Cost of Being a Negro," Sociological Inquiry 35, Number 1 (Winter 1965), pp. 41–58. Reprinted in John F. Kain (ed.), *Race and Poverty: the Economics of Discrimination,* op. cit., pp. 60–67.

Table 9-6. Subemployment Indicators[a] for Men, 1966 and 1967 (Numbers in Thousands)

	Nonwhite	White
Subemployment rate:[a]		
1966	21.6	7.6
1967[b]	c	c
Indicators of subemployment:[b]		
Number of low earners:		
1966	635	1,417
1967	505	1,176
Percent change	−31	−17
Monthly average number unemployed 15 weeks or more:[b]		
1966	69	255
1967	53	202
Percent change	−23	−21

Source. United States Department of Labor, Bureau of Labor Statistics.

[a] *The Manpower Report of the President,* issued April 1968, published a new national subemployment measure for 1966 (pp. 34–36). This measure includes (1) workers unemployed 15 weeks or more and (2) workers who made less than $3000 in 1966 for year-round full-time work (taken as a proportion of the entire labor force with a week or more of work experience during the year). This indicator is, therefore, on an annual basis and considerably different from the subemployment rate in a specific week, arrived at last year for workers in urban slums (See p. 97 in *Social and Economic Conditions of Negroes in the United States,* October 1967, BLS Report No. 332 and Current Population Reports, Series P-23, No. 24).

[b] Annual data for those unemployed 15 weeks or more in 1967 are not yet available: therefore, a rate is not computed but two subemployment indicators are given. These are not precisely the same as those required for the national subemployment rate published for 1966.

[c] Data not available.

As the majority of Negroes interviewed by *Newsweek* poll put it, "if you do the same work as a white man you will probably be paid less than he will." And now we can say how much less: about $1000 a year.[16]

The Council of Economic Advisors indicated that "if Negroes received the same average pay as whites having the same educa-

---

[16] Ibid., p. 67.

tion, the personal income of Negroes and that of the nation would have been $12.8 billion higher." In addition "if Negroes also had the same educational attainments of white workers and earned the same pay and experienced the same unemployment of whites, their personal income and that of the nation would have been $20.6 billion higher. The cumulative effect of this would hove been an estimated increase in Gross National Product of 3.7%."[17]

A. Urban Alternatives and the Ghetto[18]

The existence of racial and economic ghettos is not a new phenomenon in America's urban environment. The inner city, the circumstances of life within it, and the unrest of the urban poor have now become an integral part of the overall crisis of all large metropolitan areas. Attention was drawn to the plight of these ghetto areas by the riots of the summer of 1967. The Report of the National Advisory Committee on Civil Disorders highlighted conditions of the inner city to millions of citizens who had been oblivious to the tragedy of life within these areas. The ghettos of large urban areas with high rates of physical deterioration, diseconomies of transportation and other public services, staggering fiscal problems, and the increasing mood of psychological frustration and deterioration of the environmental quality are elements of the impending crisis in the functioning of metropolitan areas. The National Advisory Commission on Civil Disorders has identified two fundamental questions that affect the future of American cities. One, should future population be concentrated in central cities as in the past 20 years where the Negro and white populations have become even more residentially segregated? Two, should our society provide greatly increased special assistance to Negroes and other relatively disadvantaged population groups? The commission concludes that three basic questions confront the United States in the attempt to provide socially effective answers to the above questions.

---

[17] Staff memorandum of the Council of Economic Advisors (March 26, 1965, mimeographed). Reprinted as "The Economic Cost of Discrimination" in John F. Kain, *Race and Poverty*, op. cit., pp. 58–59.
[18] Pages 177–181 are drawn from William L. Henderson and Larry C. Ledebur, *Economic Disparity* (New York: Free Press, 1970), pp. 281–290.

B. The Present Policies Choice

Under the first set of alternatives, "The Present Policies Choice," the share of natural resources presently allocated to welfare effort would be maintained, with the absolute amount of welfare allocations increasing with the growth of federal revenues through time. This policy would involve simply following the present course of action. Since the present share of federal revenue allocated to antipoverty programs is insufficient even to carry out a holding action against social and economic deterioration of the inner city, the commission argues that the present policies choice does not represent a realistic solution.

At this juncture the lack of insight or understanding of the complexity and interrelatedness of the problems of the ghetto and the absence of essential research is critical. Our understanding of the dimension of the problems of interrelationships is deficient. It is critical that additional research be undertaken to increase understanding of the complexity of the issues. The imperative urgency of these problems will not allow the time necessary to undertake careful and systemmatic studies. It is necessary that some procedure be designated that will "buy" the time to complete these studies. One technique for buying time is a system of income supplements for guaranteed annual income.

The Report of the Advisory Commission on Civil Disorders points out that the present system of public welfare has contributed to the tensions and social disorganizations leading to the civil disorders of the summer of 1967. There are few familiar with the present system of social welfare that would dispute this conclusion. The system does not provide for the basic needs of the people living in poverty. The limitations of the system have created strong social tensions both among recipients of the welfare and in the larger society that provides this aid but does not understand the nature of poverty.[19]

The recommendations of the commission call for an overhaul of the present system. The changes recommended are major. They urge for some form of guaranteed annual income which would be available to all poverty categories with no categorical restrictions or qualifications.

---

[19] The Report of the President's Commission on Civil Disorders, p. 57.

The potential for some form of guaranteed annual income to eliminate the differential between actual income of those living in poverty and the incomes necessary to raise them to an acceptable standard of living depends on the size of this "poverty income gap" and its rate of elimination in the absence of programs for redistribution. The Economic Report of the President of 1969 estimates that given the rate of decrease of poor between 1961 and 1968, poverty could be eliminated within a 10-year period. If the record of 1968 could be maintained, this time span could be reduced to approximately 5½ years.[20]

However the Council of Economic Advisors points out that this reduction would be extremely hard to maintain. Those remaining in the poverty category have no direct participation in the economic system and thus will be affected only slightly by any general increase in prosperity. The average rate of increase of the income of the nonpoor is 3% per year. If the incomes of those persons in the poverty category were to increase at this same rate, 12 to 17 years would be needed to eliminate poverty. Thus action must be taken to increase the incomes of the poor more rapidly than those of the nonpoor. This can occur only through some form of redistribution of income. The Council of Economic Advisors concludes that this redistribution process can be accomplished with only small sacrifices from nonpoor income categories.

Only a relatively small redistribution of the benefits of growth is needed to speed greatly the reduction of poverty. If the approximately 85% of the households that are poor and receive about 95% of total income are willing to make only a small sacrifice of the estimated 3% yearly growth in their real income per capita, the prospects for poverty reduction could be greatly transformed. If the increase in the real income for the nonpoor is lowered, merely from 3% to 2½% per year, and that differential of about 2.8 billion dollars annually is effectively transferred to those in poverty, then family incomes for those now poor can grow about 12% annually. This redistribution would eliminate the 1967 "poverty gap of 9.7 billion dollars in less than 4 years." Since any program of redistribution would be likely to

---

[20] *Economic Report of the President* (Washington, D.C., United States Government Printing Office, 1969), p. 159.

reach some of the near poor and might raise some poor families substantially above the poverty line before others are affected, perhaps a better projection of the time required would be 6–8 years.[21]

V. GHETTO ENRICHMENT ALTERNATIVE

The second urban alternative delineated by the Commission on Civil Disorders is the "enrichment choice." This approach involves an attempt to offset the adverse effects of the continued segregation and deprivation of the ghetto, and to generate significant improvements in the environmental quality of these areas. This effort would not be designed to appreciably affect the pattern of segregation of the inner city but, instead, would be designed to build an economic base within the region, to make ghetto areas more habitable, and to reflect a greater environmental quality. Implicit to this alternative is the unstated promise that the ghetto can serve as an effective and largely self-sufficient unit for economic development, that the chaos and anarchy of the ghetto economy can be restructured to create an effective economic base within the inner city. It argues that business efforts must be directed at programs that will reach the ghetto economy. "This view recognizes that the ghetto economy is separate and that it encompasses millions of acres of urban real estate, which simply cannot be abandoned. The enrichment theory brings jobs, capital, and new entrepreneurial skills to the black slums. It corrects and builds upon what we now have—however undeveloped it may be. It does recognize inexorable patterns of discrimination in geographical segregation which reinforce the Negro poverty. The enrichment choice states that disadvantaged Negroes cannot achieve economic opportunity or power through an immediate migration into the white economy."[22]

Consider three essential weaknesses in the ghetto economy: (1) obsolete and unjust methods retail distribution; (2) inadequate sources of credits; (3) lack of business entrepreneurship.

---

[21] Ibid., p. 160.
[22] Theodore L. Cross, *Black Capitalism: Strategy for Business in the Ghetto* (New York: Atheneum Press, 1969), p. 139.

The following examples show that the enrichment approach is the only practical method of destroying these cancers of Black poverty.

1. Shopping centers, supermarkets, and discount stores have by-passed the ghetto for safer markets downtown or in suburban areas. The Negro does not use these outlets, either as a matter of choice, as in Harlem, or because of inadequate transportation, as in Watts. Plainly, it is necessary to find methods of establishing normal retail outlets in the ghetto. The integration choice would require an impractical program of bussing the Negro to Korvettes, Macy's, or the A & P in the suburb.

2. Reasonably priced credit must be made available to the Negro. The integration choice would force the Bedford Styvesant residents to go to downtown Brooklyn or Manhattan and apply at, say, a branch of Bankers' Trust Company. In time this must occur, but now a disadvantaged Black is reluctant to go into any bank—even Harlem's Negro Control Freedom National Bank. The immediate objective, therefore, is ghetto credit enrichment, which would bring Black credit to the ghetto by installing newly chartered banks and new branches of downdown banks in the Black core areas.

3. The Black economy lacks Negro entrepreneurs and capitalists. The resident of the ghetto almost never owns, as Richard Nixon stated during the election campaign of 1968, "a piece of the action." Our national policy would be to create Negro entrepreneurs as well as Negro executives. The economic integration approach would set the Negro up in business on Main Street, but he would be certain to fail because current racial attitudes would insure that the Negro entrepreneur operating in a white economy would find neither employees nor customers. The enrichment approach would establish him in business in the ghetto, where he would have employees and customers.

The enrichment theory would make sure that such needs as legal services, employment centers, family financial services, entertainment facilities, day-care, and health centers remained in the ghetto when they are needed, and were not established outside.[23]

The policies advocated are an intricate system of tax incentives and subsidies to induce businessmen to provide credit and entrepreneurial training to Black businessmen, and for banks to create credit sources for potential Negro entrepreneurers. The

---

23 Ibid., pp. 139–140.

lack of adequate capital sources is stressed as the primary detriment to creating the viable Black economic structure within the Ghetto.[24]

VI. ISSUES IN EVALUATION

A few modern civil rights organizations maintain the older and more traditional interests and jobs and training, but others have abandoned this approach. Black leaders have given ample testimony to wanting something more from the private sector than simply the opportunity for employment. The rejection has been stressed by conservative organizations as well as the Black militants.

Certainly jobs are an essential part of the cure for our urban ails, but they must not be considered the sole palative to the sickness. We had full employment of the poor under slavery. Today we want a piece of the action in the mainstream business system. The jobs now being provided by sincere and well-meaning white businesses serve only to provide a sense of slave security "that will only result in greater frustration, bitterness and rancour, destruction, and retribution in the days that lie ahead.[25]

The position of the Congress of Racial Equality is typical of the prevalent attitude of militant organizations.

Economic development takes priority over jobs *per se* at this point.

---

[24] The present federal efforts to assist in the establishment of Black Capitalism will function through a new Office of Minority Business Enterprise within the Department of Commerce established in March of 1969. The goal of this organization is to encourage minority entrepreneurship by creating sources of capital which will be available to the minority entrepreneur. The program is entitled "Project Enterprise" which is designed to establish minority enterprise small business investment companies called MESBICs. These investment companies will be sponsored by major corporations and capitalized with, at least, $150,000 of the corporate sponsor's money and $300,000 in small business administration funds. The ultimate goal is to establish 500 MESBICs that will be capable of generating one billion dollars in minority business investment. *Business Week*, November 15, 1968, p. 40.

[25] Berkley G. Burrell, from a speech presented to the Business Opportunity Workshop for Industrial Procurement, Bethpage, N.Y., May 24, 1968, p. 5.

A number of years ago our basic drive was for jobs. We have looked upon this as a way of solving the problem. We thought this was the answer. Based on the economic reality of our situation, jobs and that kind of income cannot reduce the gap, or cannot even keep it from getting any broader. We must have a part of the kind of income that comes from the possession of the tools. And the kind of income that comes from being the one who receives the dividends. Our goal is economic development based upon this rationalization. That is the only answer to keeping black people from becoming a totally dependent population.[26]

The upward path for Negroes, in the view of most black leaders, is through economic development programs, black businesses, or "black capitalism." The policy of black capitalism has received endorsement from the federal government.

If our urban ghettos are to be rebuilt from within, one of the first requirements is the development of black-owned and black-run businesses. The need is more than economic. The ownership of homes, land, and especially the productive enterprise is both symbol and evidence of opportunity and this is central to the spirit of independence on which orderly progress rests.[27]

The emphasis on black capitalism is also shared by leadership groups that espouse a social and political philosophy different from white or black moderates.

Blacks must manage to control the institutions that service their areas, as it has always been for other interest groups. There is an immediate need in such institutions as education, health, social service, sanitation, protection, fire, housing, etc. Large and densely populated black areas, especially in urban centers must have a change in status. They must become political subcolonial appendages of the state, instead of subcolonial appendages of the city. They must become more autonomous of the existing urban centers. In short, black people must be able to control basic societal instruments in social, political, and economic areas.[28]

---

[26] Kermit Scott, personal interview, CORE National Convention in Columbus, Ohio on July 8, 1968.

[27] Richard M. Nixon, "Bridges to Human Dignity," Address on the CBS radio network on April 25, 1968, pp. 9, 16.

[28] Roy Innis, National Director of CORE. Statement of the Subcommittee

The current emphasis on ghetto economic development and "Black Capitalism" implies that the ghetto can serve as a viable unit for economic development. However, a number of rather strong criticisms have been brought against the ghetto enrichment alternative. Foremost among them is that this alternative will not change the pattern of segregation in the inner city and may well result in an increasingly segregated pattern of life in metropolitan areas.

It is nothing less than a complete change in the metropolis that will solve the problems of the ghetto. Indeed it is ironic, almost cynical, the extent to which current programs ostensibly are concerned with the welfare of urban Negros, are willing to accept and are even based on the permanence of central ghettos. Thus, under every heading of social welfare legislation, education, income transfer, employment, and housing, we find programs that can only serve to strengthen the ghetto and the serious problems that it generates. Particularly these programs concentrate on beautifying the essentially ugly structure of the current metropolis and not on providing individuals with the tools necessary to break out of this structure. The shame of the situation is that viable alternatives do exist.[29]

It is argued that these gilding-the-ghetto alternatives present a high cost for the Negro and for society at large.[30] It is unlikely that the effort to establish successful black businesses, other than small retail or service firms, can prove successful. Purchasing power concentrated within the ghetto area may prove insufficient to provide a market for a commodity produced in quantities that reflect the existing economies of scale. This output cannot be competitive with products produced outside of the ghetto. Lack of adequate purchasing power within the ghetto will force the ghetto industry into competition with larger markets external

---

on Equal Opportunity in Urban Society before the Resolutions Committee, Republican National Convention, Miami Beach, Florida, July 30, 1968, pp. 6–7.

[29] John F. Kain and Joseph J. Persky, "Alternatives to the Gilded Ghetto," Program on Racial and Urban Economics, Discussion Paper 21, February 1968, pp. 18–69.

[30] William L. Henderson and Larry C. Ledebur, *Economic Disparities, Programs for the Economic Development of the Negro* (New York: The Free Press, 1970).

to the ghetto. Black enterprises then will incur competitive disadvantages.

There are no longer any strong ghetto locational factors to influence the location of any capital-intensive industry within this area. The two positive locational factors in the ghetto environment are a source of cheap unskilled labor and a relative proximity to urban markets. Technological development in transportation has greatly reduced the importance of the market proximity factor. A successful black industry must be designed to take advantage of the unique comparative advantage of the ghetto: the cheap labor supply. Any new industry must be designed to be labor-intensive to utilize a low level of skills, for example, the tent-making and bat-making endeavors of Watts. Any firms of this type must remain on a small scale. Thus there will be an extremely small impact on employment in the ghetto. The firm will ultimately be faced with the certainty of becoming less competitive with other capital-intensive industries. It is difficult to perceive black capitalism in the ghetto as a successful development option.

In addition, it may be difficult to attract established industrial operations in the ghetto areas to provide sources of jobs and incomes for ghetto residents. Private industry cannot significantly reduce ghetto unemployment without a sharp increase in costs and a consequent reduction in profits. In addition to the higher costs of training the hardcore unemployed, industries may have to redesign production processes to introduce labor-intensive low-skill rated jobs. This type of jobs is being eliminated through technological advance and automation. Reduced efficiency and other sources of high cost will occur.

The effort to create job mobility as opposed to labor mobility by locating industrial enterprises within the ghetto will also result in higher costs because of the absence of positive locational factors within these areas. Adverse locational factors within the ghetto or positive locational factors outside the ghetto are:

1. Land is cheaper outside the central city, whereas congestion is a predominant characteristic within.
2. Developments in transportation, including the growth of air and highway transportation, make it less essential for plants to be located near the hub of large cities.

3. Technological developments favor the use of single story, continuous-processing plants.

4. There is less crowding away from the central city, making it easier for employers to find housing near their work and to commute more readily.

5. The type of industry which has been growing most rapidly hires highly skilled and technically trained workers who are both attracted to and can afford the relatively improved and modern public facilities characteristic of the environment of the new suburb.[31]

If industry can only attack the problems in the ghetto, to the reduction in their profitability, the issue becomes whether they have a social responsibility to do so in spite of the effect on their profit situation, or whether the federal government should create incentives for them to do so through tax incentives or subsidies.

The question of whether tax subsidies or incentives should be created to offset the adverse locational factors of inner-city areas to entice industry to locate their operations there is complex. There exists a concensus among fiscal theorists on the usefulness and advantages of local tax-concession aid to industrial expansion. Taxes are not an important detriment of plant location, and the effect of exemptions is to complicate the fiscal affairs of the local government.

Tax concessions and low business taxes may, in fact, be a deterrent to industrial development in a locality. Businesses interested in expansion are as much concerned with government expenditure patterns as with tax structure. Expenditure patterns reflected in the standard or quality of local services in relation to tax payments typify the tax climate of the state or locality. Adequate schools, universities, highways, vocational programs, public recreation, and the expenditures for public works are factors in stimulating industrial development at the local government level. If low rates or tax exemptions do not provide adequate revenues for local services, the "favorable" tax structure may be signifi-

---

[31] Employment and Manpower Problems of the City; Implications of the Report of the National Advisory Commission on Civil Disorders, Report of the Joint Economic Committee, 90th Congress, Second Session, Washington, D.C.: Government Printing Office, 1968, p. 10.

cant in stifling industrial expansion, Efficient, adequate and reliable local services, a good planning and zoning commission, as well as honest and effective local government have been more attractive in local industrialization programs than gifts and concessions.[32]

These state, local, and federal government urban industrial subsidies, and/or tax concessions, foster criticism based on discrimination, equity, effectiveness, and efficiency in resource allocation. Ultimately, the evaluation of the effectiveness of these concessions and inducements is predicated on achieving the desired economic objectives.

It is questionable whether tax concessions and other local government industrial development schemes have made significant impact on city blight or on the size of hardcore unemployment roles. Whether or not such schemes have been effective in expanding the industrial base and/or employment and thus in creating aggregate demand is debatable. The syndrome of factors responsible for the selection of site locations and the pattern of production and hiring of new industrial facilities makes the assessment of particular detriments difficult. New industrial facilities also incur costs to governments and residents. They challenge the premise that all new industrial sites bring positive change to the economic structure of finacial environment. Generally stated, increase in aggregate demand from whatever source has not contributed significantly to improving the economic conditions of the Negro.[33]

Thus efforts to create black economic development or "black capitalism" in the ghetto are unrealistic and possess an unacceptably high risk of failure. The current emphasis on ghetto economic development and black capitalism implies that the ghetto can be a viable unit for economic development.[34] New

---

[32] See W. L. Henderson and H. A. Cameron, *The Public Economy* (New York: Random House, 1969), pp. 358–361.

[33] William L. Henderson and Larry C. Ledebur, "Government Incentives and Black Economic Development," *Review of Social Economy*, Vol. 27, No. 2, September 1969, p. 209.

[34] Pages 188 through 192 are drawn from William L. Henderson and Larry C. Ledebur, "The Viable Alternative for Black Economic Development," *Public Policy*, Vol. 18, Spring 1970, pp. 446–449.

industry in the inner city may provide sources of income for ghetto residents, and may make capital funds available for establishing black businesses that cater to a market of Negro customers. Such enrichment of the ghetto will not change the pattern of segregation in the inner city. These programs may result in increasing the segregated pattern of life in metropolitan areas.

In addition to the issue of the socially negative effect, can the ghetto serve as a viable unit for economic development?

If the prospects for ghetto industry in general are limited, the prospects for Negro-owned or Negro-operated industry—now so popular an idea—are even more so. The notion of self-help, as the constructive aspect of "black power" is inherently appealing, and Negro entrepreneurship should be encouraged . . . But . . . to suggest that Negro entrepreneurship can produce much more than a token number of new jobs for the hard-core unemployed, at least for a long time to come, is pure romanticism. Ghetto autarchy is impossible. Even if the ghetto market could be walled off, in effect, through appeals to Negros to "buy black," the market is not big enough to support significant manufacturing, and the number of white employees who could be replaced by black workers in retail and service establishments is limited. Any large-scale increase in Negro employment by Negro enterprises would have to come through those able to compete successfully with white-owned enterprises in the larger market outside the ghetto, and they are sure to develop only slowly.[35]

A. Ghetto Eradication or Dispersal

It is probable that the alternative of integration or ghetto dispersal corresponds most closely to traditional American idealism. In terms of economic viability, the dispersal approach is preferable. Militant blacks, however, object to the implications of ghetto dispersal. They argue that the Negro is building organizations and political power for the first time in ghetto centers. Any policy that would result in the erosion of this power base is suspect. In addition, militants believe that the time span necessary to achieve economic development is too slow under any

---

[35] J. L. Sundquist, "Jobs Training and Welfare for the Underclass," in *Agenda for the Nation* (Washington, D.C.: Brookings Institution, 1968), p. 58.

evolutionary dispersal policy. Integration will be gradual, and action is needed now. Militants are unwilling to see another generation of urban Negroes sacrificed to poverty. In all probability, another generation of Negroes would be passed over as a result of programs designed to achieve their social and economic acceptance in the established white residential and industrial communities.

The economic development of central urban areas may seem like a logical first step in upgrading the economic status of Negroes. But Kain and Persky, of the M.I.T.-Harvard Joint Center for Urban Studies, label any "gilding-the-ghetto" proposals as inadequate to meet the exigencies of the Negroes' economic plight. They point to the Negroes' problem as the existence of the ghetto.

It is clear that the impact of the ghetto on the processes of metropolitan development has created and aggravated many of the most crucial urban problems . . . The ghetto has isolated the Negro economically as well as socially.[36]

It may seem that we have made the ghetto too much the villain. Physical segregation may have only been the not so subtle way to avoid discriminatory practices that might else be rampant. Many ghetto problems might still exist in some other guises. Nevertheless, the problem as structured *now* must continue as long as the metropolis harbors this "peculiar instituition."[37]

The typical list of obvious ghetto problems such as unemployment, low income, poor housing, and poor schools must be supplemented by complementary problems of "distortion of metropolitan development that has added substantially to problems in the central city finance. metropolitan transportation, housing, and urban renewal." The decline of central cities has been hastened by a conviction in the white community, both individual and corporate, that the ghetto would continue its

---

[36] John F. Kain and Joseph J. Persky, *Alternatives to the Gilded Ghetto* (Program on Regional and Urban Economics, Discussion Paper No. 21, prepared for the Economic Development Administration Research Conference, United States Department of Commerce, Washington, D.C., Winter 1968), pp. 8, 9.

[37] Ibid., p. 12.

rapid expansion with the associated problems of concentrated poverty and social disorganization.[38] If this evaluation is applicable, Negro problems can be attacked most directly by eradication or dispersal of the ghetto which, in turn, will require a massive alteration or reshaping of the physical, residential, economic, and social environment of the central city.

B. The Long Run—End the Ghetto

In the long run, the subsidy theme can be carried farther as an acceptable pattern of policy development to break up the Black inner-city subculture. The ghetto dispersal concept should ultimately be implemented. Subsidies for out-migration, and other features directly affecting labor mobility are important. Moving costs to workers and training costs to existing firms outside the ghetto would be useful. Income maintenance in the form of negative income tax would probably be less costly and more effective than alternative programs for employment if they were accompanied by low-cost housing construction, new transportation facilities, industry location, and educational opportunities in satellite cities.[39]

The ghetto dispersal concept is the only strategy that promises a long-run solution. None of the economic development approaches can reduce the financial and other distortions of urban growth that have resulted from the development and expansion of city ghetto cores.

Despite the urgency of the current situation, alternative policies must be evaluated in terms of their long run impact. The selection of specific program tools should be governed by a careful definition of the underlying problems. Few existing programs have such a legitimate birth.[40]

---

[38] The characteristics and magnitude of the urban government financial crises that confirm problems noted by Kain and Persky (op. cit., p. 3) are reported in Part IV, "The Crisis of Urban Government Finance," *Report of the National Commission on Urban Problems*, pt. IV, Chapter 3 (Washington, D.C.: Government Printing Office, mimeographed).

[39] For an extended discussion of techniques for implementing the dispersal alternatives, see Henderson and Ledebur, *Economic Disparity*, Chapter 10.

[40] Kain and Persky, op. cit., p. 1.

Ghetto dispersal will probably cost less that the various gilding-the-ghetto programs. Breaking up and eliminating the ghetto is the only approach that is consistent with the stated goals of our society. Black capitalism and/or jobs within the ghetto tend to strengthen the existing segregated pattern. The ghetto dispersal strategy is not only consistent with the nation's long-run goals but will be substantially cheaper.[41]

The ghetto dispersal alternative is the only procedural way to eliminate the ingredients of potential economic disaster. The number of jobs in the ghetto cannot expand because of the limitations on revenue from any increased sales activities. Meanwhile public service requirements will expand and with increased costs. Increased cost of all public services will cause both businessmen and public agencies to consider moving out of the inner city to places of lower costs and density. Urban cores will be even more depleted of jobs and leadership. If the present pattern of economic growth continues, employment opportunities for the indigenous resident will shrink. The quality of services offered would be reduced, while the nonghetto economy as a whole would progress.[42]

The existing economic conditions of the metropolitan structure function detrimentally for the poverty group, now, and the syndrome of factors will continue to develop even more negatively.[43] The dispersal of the ghetto is the only policy that retains any hope of allowing the United States to achieve the social cohesiveness essential to sustain society in its present institutional form. The challenges of implementing the dispersal alternative should be the primary focus for remedial development programs. The goal of achieving the reconstruction of the ghetto and integration of the Negro into the larger white society must be

---

[41] See John Kain and Joseph Persky, *Alternatives to the Gilded Ghetto,* op. cit., pp. 18–32.

[42] See William J. Baumol, "Macro-Economics of Unbalanced Growth: The Anatomy of Urban Crisis," *American Economic Review,* June 1967, 415–426; and K. W. Deutsch and R. L. Meier, *The Confederation of Urban Government: How Self-Controls for the American Megalopolis Can Evolve,* Working Paper No. 77, Center for Planning and Development Research, University of California, Berkeley, June 1968, p. 7.

[43] *Conference of Urban Government,* p. 7.

the primary criterion for evaluating all development and incentive programs. "The best future strategy appears to be that of choosing policies which increase the wealth-producing capabilities of the metropolitan areas as a whole, by making it more attractive to new enterprise and professionals, while simultaneously working out a means of bargaining between member communities so as to distribute an increasing flow of public funds in an equitable way."[44]

The Negro in this country clearly faces a broad range of pressing problems. Problems that challenge the basic structure of our social and physical environment. While there are many proposals and counter proposals aimed at the ultimate solution, it is clear now that no easy way out exists.[45]

---

[44] Ibid. p. 48.
[45] Kain and Persky, op. cit., p. 1.

10

The Dilemma and Future of the City

The metropolitan milieu should be perceived as dynamic phenomena. A static interpretation of city problems and policies within only contemporary parameters results in inexorable planning that attempts to interdict social, economic, and technological forces. Rigid planning or urban design cannot be responsive to the dynamic of urban change. Static and rigid approaches cause regeneration of a cycle of increasing urban problems.

The urbanologist should understand the dynamics of the urban environment and should project the image of what the city could become as its functions alter, deteriorate, and are renewed in response to (a) the decline of the strong nineteenth and twentieth century centralizing forces, (b) new and intensified changes in market forces, (c) technological innovation, and (d) social innovation.

Social innovation may be the single most critical variable in man's creative vision of the vital city. The issues of what the city will become in form and function and what the city should be as man's control over his environment increases are of more long-range significance than current urban problems.

A. The Efficacy of the Price Mechanism

The city is a complex, interrelated social system. Multiple variables interact within the city. The range and magnitude of these variables are so complex that they cannot be assimilated by the human mind.

. . . the human mind is not adapted to interpreting how social systems behave. Our social systems belong to a class called multi-loop, non-linear, feedback systems. In the long history of evolution it has not been necessary for man to understand these systems until the very recent historical times. Evolutionary processes have not given us the mental skill needed to properly interpret the dynamic behavior of systems of which we have now become a part.[1]

Thus it is necessary to attempt to understand the nature of the city as an interrelated social system which in its entirety cannot be assimilated.

Given a social system of the city, the question of most significance is what monitors and regulates the system to insure the most beneficial interaction for the "social good." There must be some decision-making procedure that will determine the final configuration of the interaction of all variables. The question more succinctly stated is "What is or should be the decision making procedure within the complex social system such as the city?"

Several alternatives have application:

1. The anarchistic solution or anarchy, where the rule of power prevails. Individuals or coalitions of individuals with the greatest coercive power thus would insure that the final outcome of interaction would conform to their particular value patterns or desires. Hopefully, society in view of man's fallibility, has moved to a level of civilization in which solutions based on the coercive power are no longer a reality.

2. A "social welfare" or "superman value function" or an accepted list of social priorities as a base of reference for the allocation of resources in the final configuration of goods, services and activities. Again, a problem arises because there is little agreement about what a city should be, or on urban goals and priorities (see page 10, Chapter 1). This problem is illustrated in the example of the "analogy of games." The problem of variegated social evaluation within the urban environment is analogous to a football field with simultaneous games of football, soccer, baseball, and basketball. The multiplicity and conflict of values

---

[1] Jay W. Forrester, "Counterintuitive Behavior of Social Systems," *Technology Review*, January 1971, p. 53.

and rules generate a complex situation that requires an extensive arbitration of the disparity in rules. In a city, there are many "games" enacted under different values, premises, and rules. A referee or some mechanism is necessary to arbitrate the interaction and to resolve conflicts to determine a final best configuration for that social system.

3. A third possibility may become feasible in the future with advancements in physical and social technology. Computers can interrelate many variables and can provide determinate solutions from some maximizing principle. The obvious problem is the capacity of contemporary computers to record the plethora of variables and parameters which interact throughout the city. The computer is constrained in capacity by the complexity of programs, and the data it can store. An additional difficulty, although not a limitation of the computer, is the large number of input variables that must be incorporated, but that cannot be identified, or quantified. As man's technology, both social and physical improves, it may be possible to overcome these limitations.

4. There is a mechanism within the urban environment analogous to a computerized system designed to achieve some programmed goal. The pricing mechanism is a system through which countless simultaneous and successive iterations interrelate quantitative variables under a minimizing rule,—the rule of profit. The price system makes allocative decisions for vital goods and services, resources, and the distribution of industry and people throughout the city. Marginal calculations determine the most valued use as measured by money equivalents of urban resources. For example, the pricing mechanism determines the allocation of urban space in the following manner (Figure 10–1).

Assume that there are four alternative employments for urban land. The spatial demand for land in these uses are represented by demand curves A, B, C, and D. These demand curves are reflective of the value of the land in its alternate use and represent the ability to bid it away from competing uses. Thus land segment 1 would be utilized in employment A, land segment 2 should be utilized in alternative B, and so forth. The market mechanism, therefore, allocates urban space to that use in which it has the greatest social utility. This again assumes that the value

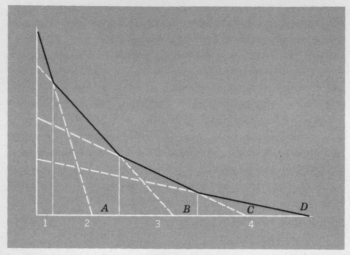

Figure 10–1. Alternative demand for urban land.

of all competing uses can be measured by the numeraire of money and made effective in the market.

Throughout this book the disciplinary force of the urban pricing mechanism has been emphasized as fundamentally important. No other available mechanism is more capable of handling the complex interaction of variables or of providing a solution with an identifiable maximizing principle. It is extremely important to the ongoing function of the urban economy and social system that a mechanism exist which can successfully arbitrate and adjudicate conflicting values, claims, and demands on urban resources and functions.

Thus the urban price system is a necessary mechanism. Not all decisions stemming from this mechanism produce the most desirable or the best obtainable results within the city.

I. URBAN MARKET LIMITATIONS

There are two basic limitations to the final allocation derived through the market process.

1. The allocation derived from the pricing mechanism is socially best, only if it is assumed that distribution of income is

socially desirable. All men could compete in the marketplace with relative effective purchasing power if there is a desirable distribution of income. Income distribution introduces inequalities in the ability of individuals to make their market preferences effective.

2. Using the analogy of the market mechanism as a computer, the results of decision making are only as good or socially desirable as the data fed into the market. If data on variables are not obtainable (that is, intangible costs and benefits or nonquantifiable preferences) or if incorrect data are utilized (that is, significant external costs and benefits or artificial distortions of market data resulting from interdiction into the market), the resulting social configuration will not be the best.

The use of the computer-market analogy identifies two important policy options.

1. The option to improve the quantity and quality of the data that work through the market mechanism. This would involve policies to insure that external costs and benefits are included in the functioning market mechanism (see Chapter 5). Quasi-public and public goods must be priced in a market so that economic entities reflect rational decisions on their allocation and consumption (see Chapter 6). It is difficult to readjust market data to reflect true costs and benefits of intangibles. However, this policy choice has not received careful consideration other than by professional economists.

2. The second major policy option is to readjust the final configuration originally determined by the market to produce more socially desirable results. Attempts to readjust the final configuration have been made in welfare programs, subsidized or public housing programs, public transportation, job training programs, job placement programs, and urban government fiscal policy.

This policy option is more readily perceived and is utilized more extensively than the preceding option. Its implementation is easier but there is great danger of adverse results. Public policy which is designed to adjust this configuration . . . of output of goods and services requires finely tuned policy tools plus the capacity to make incremental adjustments. Such policy tools, because of the lack of appropriate data and the lags of policy implementation, are not refined enough to produce desired reallocations. The limitations in policy mechanisms to permit refined marginal adjustments are a salient limitation in current public policy. The counter-intuitive elements of a complex social system indicate that it may be easy to intuitively identify reallocative policies, but such policies introduce distortions and potentially adverse results.

For the last several decades the country has slipped into a set of attitudes about our cities that are leading to actions that have become an integral part of the system that is generating greater troubles. If we were malicious and wanted to create urban slums, trap low-income people in ghetto areas, and increase the number of people on welfare, we could do little better than follow the present policies. The trend toward stressing income tax and sales tax and away from the real estate tax encourages old buildings to remain in place and blocks self-renewal. The concessions in income tax laws to encourage low-income housing will in the long run actually increase total low income population in the country. The highway expenditures and the government loans for suburban for higher income groups to abandon urban areas than to revive them. The pressures to expand the areas incorporated by urban government in an effort to expand the revenue base, have been more than offset by lowered administrative efficiency, more citizen frustration, and the accelerated decline that is triggered in the annexed areas. The belief that more money will solve urban problems has taken the tension away from correcting the underlying causes and has instead allowed the problems to grow to the limit of available money, whatever the amount might be.[2]

II. URBAN POLICY ALTERNATIVES

This book identifies selected policy issues within the urban environment: (1) the microeconomic functions of the city, the allocation of resources, and final goods and services through space and time, (2) the macroeconomics of the city, the division of economic functions among cities, the hierarchy of cities, and the input and output matrices of the urban environment, (3) situations in which the market system fails to provide for the most efficient allocation of urban resources, (4) the demand and supply of public goods, their market and nonmarket parameters,

---

[2] Jay Forester, "Counter Intuitive Behavior of Social Systems," ibid., p. 59.

(5) public finance and urban environment, (6) the preeminent problem of the provision of adequate housing in the urban society, (7) the problem of providing for the flow of persons and commodities spatially through the city, the question of traffic and traffic congestion, (8) the problem of essential welfare within the city, and the question of urban poverty, slums, and ghettos.

The basic policy problem in all of these issues is how the pricing mechanism operates. Problem-solving urbanologists identify this policy issue in three specific subcategories:

1. Urban functions that must be sustained and in which the pricing mechanism works efficiently to achieve socially desirable results. The microeconomic function of allocation of economic activities through space is performed better through the pricing mechanism than through centralized planning or allocative policy. The conclusion can be sustained that situations such as zoning where the pricing mechanism has been interdicted results in enlarged, unfortunate consequences for the urban environment. Other attempts to interdict a market determination of housing supply and traffic have also produced unfortunate allocations consequences. More favorable alternatives can be implemented that are more complimentary to the decision-making process of the pricing mechanism. Public policy should focus on the question of urban housing and traffic, but policy decisions should reflect the directions determined by the pricing mechanism. Probably, a final configuration derived from the market priority would be more socially preferable.

There are, however, cases where the pricing mechanism cannot achieve desirable results. Since our policy tools are unrefined and clumsily designed, the correction of the market distortions obtained through the pricing mechanism is problematical in these areas.

2. The second category relates to situations where the market cannot establish prices or where the pricing mechanism cannot provide the allocation of resources under the efficiency criterion. Example cases with externalities, social costs, or benefits, militate against the effectiveness of the market mechanism. The case of public goods or quasi-public goods where there are significant nonmarket parameters also falls within this category.

The choice of one of the dual policy alternatives, (1) improving data quantification in the existing market system, or (2) adjusting final output configuration, is critical. Cost and benefits not presently quantified can be priced, and the market system can be relied on to produce a desirable configuration. Where this is a possibility, the desirable policy option would be to attempt to rely on the market. In other cases with significant nonquantifiable or intangible variables (the aesthetic and recreational), policy interdiction must adjust the final market configurations. In either choice the difficulties and the counter-intuitive elements or alternatives should be carefully examined and understood.

3. The final urban policy category applies when the pricing mechanism produces socially undesirable results (see Chapter 1, pages 3 to 5). The problem of personal alienation and anonymity, the crisis in essential welfare, the crisis in urban environmental quality, and the problems created by interdependence in the urban environment are within the category of market failure or the inability to achieve socially desirable results. Of these only the question of environmental quality can be approached by attempting to improve the data input in the market environment. In the others the policy alternative must adjust the final configuration of the price mechanism to move toward more socially desirable results.

III. THE DILEMMA OF THE CITY

The fundamental dilemma in the urban environment is deciding which organizing principles can or should be effective within the city to determine the allocation of lands, goods, and services and to arbitrate the economic interactions among persons. The importance of the pricing mechanism has been identified. No other mechanism can presently substitute for it in the city. Historically, market-oriented ideology has been primary to social organization in the United States. The dilemma is that the pricing mechanism is necessary, but market-oriented allocation alone results in an economic city. Do we want an economic city?

To admit the necessity for price allocation in the city, or to argue that an economic city is desirable, is a type of economic determinism. This determinism is based on the assumption that economic efficiency will produce a social system or city that is best or is at least, the best obtainable. To sustain this position, it is necessary to demonstrate that basic social objectives such as human welfare, health, beauty, community, environmental design, aesthetic quality, and maximum free choice result from market interactions. The dimensions of human values cannot be measured in monetary terms and are exclusive of the market system. The only recourse is to alter the final market output configuration through conscious and explicit planning.

Reallocation, planning, and design is needed to insure basic human objectives. The market allocation system fails in a massive way with respect to human fulfillment. Thus the imperative of planning and design is a logical corollary of urban social welfare. There must be a greater centralization of decision-making authority within the urban environment if the city is to respond to the current and future challenges. Technology and the increasing scale and complexity of the social system of the city create a need for greater decision-making centralization at a time of increasing psychological need for a sense of autonomy or control over the forces that determine individual life styles. This conflict will continue to underlie the problem of the city and will exacerbate the difficulty of achieving a city in which basic human objectives can be obtained.

IV. PLANNING FOR WHAT?

It is easy to generalize on the human and social objectives that should be the goals of urban planning and design, that is, the creation of community, the creation of a high level of environmental quality and aesthetics in which the physical surrounding and structure reinforce man in the process of becoming; a social system in which the loving human encounter is joined, and which is a cradle of all that is best in man's culture and civilization. To give content to these generalities in terms of understanding the effects of the environmental and physical structure on individual man, or man as a creature in society, is a very difficult task.

We know a great deal about what a city should not be from

historical experience and from observations about the social effects of design. Urban planning is advancing rapidly in its capacity to design physical environments that avoid social and human degradation and that compensate for a laisse-faire policy of urban development. It is not sufficient to understand only what the city *should not* be. But we know little about what the city should be. The relationship between physical form, structure and design, and the basic human objectives in social systems is poorly understood. We do not know what forms of social organization or which structural forms enhance the possibilities of achieving individual or societal objectives.

For example, there is a need for man to achieve a sense of community and responsibility to the society as a whole. But beyond this we do not know what the nebulous concept of community is or how to achieve it. It is difficult to derive a definition of community. Given a definition, we fail to understand how physical form contributes to it. The disciplines of psychology and social psychology have not provided useful information on the effects of density and proximity of population within the complex social system on man, the individual. Experiments on laboratory rodents indicate the detrimental affects of high density. It is dangerous to compare the results of experiments on animals to man. Although little is known about man, one pervading characteristic is recognized. Man's high degree of adaptability exceeds that observed in animals. Another dimension of man that must be assessed is the need for access to aesthetic and natural resources. Is the need for beauty and access to open space and resources biologically based, or is it acculturated? If the answer is acculturation, many of the conclusions about urban planning and design are misleading.

In the absence of a more satisfactory organizing principle, the price mechanism must be relied on to perform many functions within the urban environment. The operation of this mechanism will provide for an economic city predicated on the rationality of efficiency. If the market fails, or is ineffective, the urban decision-making processes must be interdicted so that policies do not produce conflict with inexorable technological and economic forces but, instead, provide an increase in the general welfare at a minimum cost in adverse allocation distortions. However, the market will fail to achieve certain basic human objectives such as a highly developed sense of community and the provision of environmental aesthetics within the physical structure. The recognition of the need for planning and design indicates only a direction for research and study, not how a social system can be developed that provides for or reinforces an environment in which Lewis Mumford's "Loving Human Encounter" will occur.

A. The Post-City Age

From its inception in the Tigris-Euphrates River valley to the establishment of the modern metropolis, the city has been a highly functional organization. The nature of its function has changed through time. Early cities served as centers of defense, religious activity, culture, and commerce and trade. The defense and religious roles of the cities became secondary in the period of nation building and during the Industrial Revolution. Cities then played a functional economic role as "centers" for production and for the distribution of goods and services and as locales of skilled and specialized labor, when technological advances required the specialization of the labor.

Cities through history have retained a cultural orientation, despite the fact that technological advances and cultural changes make most urban functions obsolete. The persistent function is culturally related. In a future post-city age the city may become less of a purely functional organization structure.

The existence of cities today is threatened by the disappearance of their traditional reasons, which largely determine their historical forms. Far from offering a means of defense against enemies, cities are particularly vulnerable to attack. Cities have no monopoly on trade as they had when medieval markets flourished. People are not obliged to live in cities because the only jobs are there, or because transportation is lacking to allow them to live elsewhere. No city has a cultural monopoly; these are the days of mass media and the search for original music, theatre, dance, takes one not merely to the central city, but to many cities, suburbs, and summer festival centers, and ubiquitous transportation has led to the city that, Wright's broadacre city, is everywhere and nowhere. Our cities are formed not by necessity and tradition like the design of the Navajo blanket, but by discipline, desire and design.

If we are to have cities, I suggest, it must be because they make men. To do this our cities must be more attractive, more socially agreeable, offer higher standards of comfort and convenience, better opportunities for exchanging ideas and experiences, as well as goods, and hold more beauty than other possible ways of life. In ever new ways, they must be strong magnets, vital centers. The reason for living in the city, or going there at all, as many since Aristotle have observed, is that it offers a new way of life.[3]

Many factors contribute to the diminution of the centralized pull of urban areas in the United States: (a) the problems of aging, (b) the diseconomies of scale, such as congestion, (c) declining environmental quality, (d) rising crime rates, and the like. Major forces of urban decentralization are related to the phenomenal advance of science and technology. Technological progress may be removing all restrictions on urban form and design, that is, architecturally, spatially, schematically and functionally. The effects of technological advance now appear in communication, transportation, and the rate of automation in United States industry.

V. TECHNOLOGY AND COMMUNICATIONS

Advances in transportation and production technology plus the changing structural demand of our resources are creating cities that are not industrial centers. Some cities are now centers for the production of services and information relating to intellectual, management, financial, and educational expertise. "Our society cannot function without accurate and timely information, and our largest, most important cities are those which are major communication systems . . . . to put it simply: cities are communications systems."[4]

Cities as places of informational expertise and communication systems play very different roles than traditionally assigned to urban areas.

No potential urban dweller can remain oblivious to the ad-

---

[3] Frederick Gutheim, "Urban Space and Urban Design," pp. 127–28.
[4] Ron Abler, "What Makes Cities Important," *Bell Telephone Magazine*, March-April 1970, p. 12.

vances in communications and electronics or impervious to their impact on society and the individual. Examples are the expanding use of the telephone as a communications device, the increased use of direct telephone ties and the possibility of telephones that will communicate visual as well as audio messages, the phenomenal growth of television in the postwar era, the creation of colored image patterns, the use of closed-circuit television by industry, the possibilities of recording and delayed playback television images, the phenomenal advance of computer technology, the use of computers for data assimilation, retrieval, assessment, and decision-making, and the extensive computer tie-ins throughout the nation. Telecommunications through electronic media have created a nation that is linked with near-zero time lags in communication. The frictional cost of space in communications is being rapidly eliminated.

If the role of cities is to be informational specialization, advances in electronic media communication can eliminate the need for the concentration of industries and persons. Through electronic media, information and intellectual expertise can be available everywhere and "a new set of places will become the most important locations in the national urban system. Information and ideas ore ubiquitous, there is no longer a single best place for management activities."[5]

VI. TRANSPORTATION

Transportation technology certainly has not kept pace with the rapid advancement in telecommunications. Transportation remains one of the major problems of the urban environment. The difficulty of transporting physical objects through space is much greater than that of transmitting sound waves. It is evident that there has been significant progress in transportation techniques during the first seven decades of the twentieth century. The nineteenth century core-stereotype city grew because of the limited means and high cost of transporting goods and people. A strong centralizing pull was created because transport costs within the older city were high relative to the cost of moving people. This

---

[5] Ibid., p. 15.

relative cost pattern played a critical role in the emergence of the core-dominated city.

The growth in the aeronautical sciences and the improvement in rail transit have produced a reduction in cost of time and money in transporting goods and persons through space. Thus the change in the relative costs of transporting people versus goods may amplify the trend toward dispersal of persons from the central city and from urban areas. If the problems of poverty and the attraction of the city to rural inhabitants in the poverty category are deleted from the data, a very important dispersal trend is observed. It is probable that the dispersal tendencies permitted by existing transportation modes will continue. There will be continued improvement in transportation technology.

As transportation and communication modes develop, "The standard of living which was previously only available in cities may now be enjoyed in rather remote locations, which are characterized by a much higher level of environmental amenities."[6]

VII. INDUSTRIAL TECHNOLOGY

There are dissenting views about the rate of technological advance in industry and the advance of automated techniques of production. Scholars with utopian inclinations believe that the rate of automation will increase dramatically resulting in a cybernated industrial system, or one with extensive automated machinery monitored by computerized systems and that are capable of making decisions, providing feedback, and altering elements of the production process.

Other scholars do not believe that the cybernated state is possible in the immediate future. However, industry, which is capital intensive, will utilize less labor and more technically skilled labor inputs. There will be a reduced need for large urban labor pools if industry is operated by an elite of specialists. The increasing capital intensity and automation and the con-

---

[6] John McHale, "Future Cities: Notes on a Typology," *The Futurist*, October 1969, pp. 126–130.

comitant diminution of large pools of labor will have three important effects on the urban environment.

1. Transportation and communications will reduce the need to be in cities except when immediate access to areas of concentrated consumer demand is needed. Industry will locate in response to other locational influences such as environmental quality and access to other amenities. Using the most optimistic projections of professional futurists, the possibility is created that industries and smaller communities may move to a position of semilocal economic autonomy and self-sufficiency. The fulfillment of the utopian dream may occur despite the fact that it has continuously been dashed on the necessities of economic realities.

2. Given the diminishing requirement for labor in the productive process, the problems of income distribution will be even more critical. There will be an increasing need to break the link between productivity and income and, hence, between a spatial place and income. Income redistribution forms such as the guaranteed annual income or similar programs to redistribute wealth so that all persons receive a share of capital income may be developed. Such new approaches may prove difficult to implement given our historical mores and institutional philosophies.

3. The average American male spends approximately 69% of his lifetime in the home and the female 83%, for a national average of 76% of time spent in the home. Only 24% is spent away from home. The average American spends 36% of his total time sleeping, 20% working, and 10% eating, dressing, and bathing. He is left with 1/3 of his life for "leisure, pleasure, thought, reflection, etc. This 1/3 period differentiates the quality of life."[7]

The increasing availability of leisure time may become the predominant crisis of Western culture and the variable that defines the future functions of the city.

Contemporary man may not possess the knowledge nor capacity to utilize leisure in a regenerative way, but may dissipate leisure in time-filling activities. Leisure, if it is to fill man's

---

[7] Constantine Doxiodus, in R. Eels (ed.), *Man in the City of the Future*, McMillan (New York, 1969).

psychic needs, must be productive and regenerative, not hedonistic, or pleasure oriented, or oriented toward immediate gratification. Productive leisure should become the creative use of time. Activities that are productive of the good of civilization—the political activities of participatory democracy, the cultural, social, and aesthetic goals of society—are creative of man and his community. With productive leisure and the diminishing centralization of economic functions, the implications for the city are clearer. Our urban environments will become centers for the political, educational, cultural, recreational, and aesthetic activities of our society.

The concomitant conclusion derived is that more diversity of facilities must exist that are specialized to age, income, occupational mix, and a wide range of life styles. There is an increasing need for a greater range of variety in life-styles from which people may choose, plus an increasing psychological need for a sense of autonomy and control over the forces that affect individuals' lives. Issues such as diversity and autonomy are key elements in future urbanization.

The trend in cities seems to be in the opposite direction. Urban cultures tend to be homogenous. The visible differences between places is disappearing. Cynics argue that in our urban environment, variety is dissipated. Furthermore, allegiance to city and state is weakened because of the increased mobility and the declining importance of local functions. National allegiance survives because it has stronger functional characteristics.

And in all our thinking about the future, there needs to be a more rigorous acceptance of the full range of human idiosyncratic requirements. The antiseptic and well lighted place characteristic of much current city planning practice certainly does not accommodate the diversity of human desires and preclude these. Planning for those who fall out of the normal range is relegated to the consideration of how to control deviants and avoid seaminess of bohemias and bar strips. Yet a considerable measure of "aberrance" may be expected in any human group. To plan only for the control and surveillance of those areas of human behavior which do not accord with present norms is not oriented to the future, but to the past.[8]

---

[8] John McHale, op. cit., p. 130.

Given the predictions that the need for city economic functions will diminish, and that there will be an increasing psychological need for diversity and autonomy, urban planners must devise a greater range of distinctive urban types. The opportunity costs of the cities as multi-functional entities instead of as unique areas where comparative advantage produces specialized services will be increasingly higher.

Specialization now exists in some urban areas. For example, cities serve as the focus for national and state political activities, for the educational function of a center of learning, or for entertainment activities (such as Las Vegas, Nevada and Miami, Florida).

The typology of cities for the future has interesting future implications:[9]

1. *The ceremonial city.* It would serve the functions of a political and administrative center of different levels of government throughout space.

2. *The university city.* It would provide the location for a concentration of those resources directed toward the function of learning. This type city would include the human resources in the form of teachers, massive concentration of recorded knowledge of man, the concentration of the most advanced technology of communication of knowledge and learning, and those physical facilities that are necessary to support these educational functions.

3. *The scientific city.* In this city the most advanced technological research equipment and research minds and facilities would congregate.[10]

4. *The festival or arts city.* A city of this kind is most likely to be traditional or to become a cultural and aesthetic center. Examples are Edinburgh, Venice, Salzburg, and some specific areas of existing urban centers, for example, those that have revived specific historical urban areas to exploit their tourist attractiveness.

5. *The recreation or fun city.* It would have the specialized production of recreative activities both cultural and physically

---

[9] McHale, op. cit., pp. 4–5.
[10] Ibid., p. 4.

regenerative. Centers of this kind would specialize in the production of vacation and leisure opportunities for man.

6. *The communications city.* This city would have the techniques for mass communication that are presently dispersed throughout most urban areas. Television, radio, newspapers, advertising, publishing, and some specialized consulting activities would characterize these centers. New York presently is the best approximate model of a communications city, but the rapid advancement in communication technology will create opportunities for a purer form of specialization.

7. *The convention or conference city.* It would be an urban area specialized in urban environments that serve as centers for the coming together at discreet points in time of persons with mutual interests.

8. *The museum city, or the city of history.* Examples of types of the "Museum City" are Florence, Burgess, Rome, Athens, and Williamsburg. "Within the Museum City, the future tourist may be able to adopt a life style required for actual living in the past. The Museum City or the restored archeological site becomes a kind of cycle-physical time machine with which the individual or group may reinact or reexperience the past, as in Williamsburg, or in castles, monastaries and ancient prisons or fortifications used as tourist hotels, or in the European 'Vacation in the Stone Age' plans—adult extension study courses in neolithic crafts."[11]

9. *The experimental city.* This city would offer unique opportunities in types of life-styles. "We need, even more, cities where people may go to experiment socially—different life styles, different kinds of social relationships, with varied tempos of living and possibilities of many innovative life strategies with which they may not otherwise try out."[12]

Whether these idealistic, functionally oriented, cities can produce the essential structure and ingredients for the good city of the future is debatable. But the important future issue is whether human adaptation to urban conditions, regardless of city structure or function, enhances the quality and the experience of

---

[11] Ibid., p. 130.
[12] Ibid., p. 130.

living. The emphasis on the better future in the urban environment explicitly recognizes that many elements of the existing structure and pattern of urban life are anachronistic.

There are reasons for pessimism about the capacity of society to deal effectively with current or future urbanization. There are also reasons for optimism and hope about the future good life in cities. Moreover encouraging signs indicate that fundamental problems have been recognized and that resources have been allocated to redress current urban challenges. It may now be apparent that cities are not temporary habitats to be abused and abandoned. Additional evidence shows that more resources must be channeled to redevelop and embellish urban environments. There is also the necessary recognition that the primary function of the city in the future is the positive promotion of human good.[13]

We are realizing, belatedly, that a sense of community is not a synthetic product to be created by a skillful agency employing a variety of appeals. The sense of community requires, above all, the fact of communities; an environment of direct human interdependence.[14]

---

[13] See Jeanne R. Lowe, *Cities In A Race With Time,* (New York: Vintage Books, Random House, 1968), p. 576.

[14] E. J. Mishan, *Technology and Growth: The Price We Pay,* (New York: Praeger Publishers, 1970), p. 153.

Index